D0257544

THE
PUPPY
LISTENER

Understanding and caring for your new puppy

JAN FENNELL

HARPER

HARPER

an imprint of
HarperCollins*Publishers*
77–85 Fulham Palace Road,
Hammersmith, London W6 8JB

www.harpercollins.co.uk

First published in 2010 by HarperCollins*Publishers*

Some material previously published as part of
The Seven Ages of Your Dog, HarperCollins 2005

1 3 5 7 9 10 8 6 4 2

© Jan Fennell 2010

Jan Fennell asserts the moral right to
be identified as the author of this work

A catalogue record of this book is
available from the British Library

ISBN 978-0-00-741378-2

Mixed Sources

Product group from well-managed
forests and other controlled sources
www.fsc.org Cert no. SW-COC-001806
© 1996 Forest Stewardship Council

FSC is a non-profit international organisation established to promote the
responsible management of the world's forests. Products carrying the FSC
label are independently certified to assure consumers that they come
from forests that are managed to meet the social, economic and
ecological needs of present and future generations.

Find out more about HarperCollins and the environment at
www.harpercollins.co.uk/green

THE
PUPPY
LISTENER

I dedicate this book to the dogs I have had the joy of sharing my life with, and thank them for their patience which made it possible for me to really understand them

CONTENTS

INTRODUCTION

For sheer joy and excitement, there is nothing quite like a new puppy. The pleasure these bouncing, bright-eyed balls of energy can bring into your life is immense, beyond words at times. I know this from personal experience.

As someone who has been surrounded by dogs since an early age, I've been lucky enough to have shared my life with dozens of puppies. They have come in all shapes and sizes, all sorts of breeds, and they have all been memorable canine characters. Many of them have provided me with some of my happiest memories as a dog owner.

As anyone who has ever owned a puppy knows, however, introducing a young dog into your home is never, ever easy. In fact it can be the precise opposite of that – it can be hard work. A puppy's energy and exuberance can produce mayhem if let loose in the wrong direction, as any dog owner who has witnessed a hyper-active pup run amok in their living room will testify.

So it's been no surprise to me that, ever since I began helping owners to understand and communicate with their canine companions more than a decade ago, puppies have always been high on the agenda. Indeed, while running my courses, offering consultations or giving talks around the world, questions about living with puppies arise more often than any other dog-related issues. Owners want to know about every aspect of puppy ownership: from choosing a new dog to introducing it to the home, from vaccinating to worming, grooming to training.

The answers to their diverse questions vary, of course, but there is always a common thread. Almost always I discover that the roots of any problems lie in the fact that owners have made mistakes at the beginning of their lives with their puppies. They have got off to the wrong start.

In their defence, I have to say that it is very easy to go wrong. The first six months are, without doubt, the most important in a young dog's life, and they are also the most challenging for an owner. For all their innocence and pure charm, puppies are not as straightforward as they seem.

SHOW ME THE DOG OF SIX MONTHS ...

Comparing the age of a dog to that of a human is not straightforward. The old rule of thumb that one dog year is equivalent to seven human years isn't really accurate. But it is safe to say that the first six months of a puppy's life is roughly the equivalent of between four and seven human years. In other words, it's a significant part of their life.

Think how important these years are in forming a young child's personality. 'Show me the boy of seven and I will show you the man,' the old saying goes, and it is the same with a puppy. Show me a puppy of six months old, and I will show you the dog it is going to become. This is why this period is so crucial for you, the dog owner.

Good dog ownership is always about getting off to the right start, no matter how old your new dog, but this is especially true with puppies. Your puppy needs to learn to eat, sleep and go to the toilet properly. It needs to learn how and when to play, how to interact with its human companions and – crucially – how to listen to those companions when required. Most importantly of all, it must understand its place in the human world in which it lives. And it must know how to accept you, its owner, as the leader of its domestic pack.

The lessons a puppy learns during these six months will remain with it for the rest of its life. They will dictate what kind of dog it will become in adulthood. So if you, as an owner get things right now, you will be able to look forward to a happy, contented and hopefully long relationship with your new dog. If you get them wrong, on the other hand, your problems are only just beginning.

This book is a guide to the first six months of your puppy's life. It will tell you what is going on physically and mentally in the dog's body and mind and it will take you step-by-step through the important stages you, as an owner, will have to deal with – in particular, from eight weeks of age when the vast majority of you will be taking charge of your new puppy.

Of course, there is nothing more exhilarating and life-affirming than spending time with the buoyant force of fun-loving nature that is a puppy. Puppyhood should be a time for both dog and owner to enjoy their lives together. Not to do so would be a crime! So there is also plenty of information about how to play and have fun with your puppy too. I hope this book helps you make sure that life is as long and happy as it possibly can be.

Jan Fennell, Lincolnshire, October 2010

1 | WHAT IS A DOG?

To communicate with your puppy properly you need to understand what makes it tick. And to understand that, you must first understand the answer to what might seem like a simple question: what is a dog? The answer is more complicated than you might imagine. But it will explain everything you need to know about the animal that is about to become your new best friend.

Of all the animals on earth, the dog is by far man's oldest and closest domestic partner. Our remarkable friendship dates back some 14,000 years. It was around then, so scientists believe, that wolves were first taken in by humans living in early communities. It was a good deal for both sides, as they both got something out of the new alliance. Wolves provided humans with their superior senses, which gave them an early warning system as well as powerful hunting and tracking abilities. Man provided their new partners with easy access to that precious commodity, food.

As the wolf learned to live in close proximity to humans, it evolved into a different kind of animal. It no longer had to rely on hunting and killing other animals for food. It amended its behaviour to gain acceptance in human society. As its diet changed from raw meat to human leftovers, its skull and teeth became smaller relative to the rest of its body. Its brain shrank too. Slowly the wolf became the first species to be domesticated by mankind. The wild animal became a tame one; *Canis lupus* became *Canis familiaris*.

In the thousands of years that have passed since then, selective breeding on the part of man has turned the dog into the most varied species on the planet. If dogs had been left to survive in the natural world, they would have evolved very little. Instead, over the centuries man has crossbred dogs with different traits and talents, creating what are in effect hybrids. And these dogs have reflected the different physical demands, as well as the aesthetic tastes and fashions, of humans through the ages and around the world.

THE MAIN GROUPS OF DOG

Dogs have been bred to specialise in a variety of roles, from running down prey to retrieving shot birds, from guarding houses to acting as guides for blind people.

Their DNA, and even their basic skeletal structure, remains identical to that of the wolf. But the several hundred different breeds of dog that now exist come in every conceivable shape, size and design. And while some dogs, such as the Siberian Husky or Alaskan Malamute, closely resemble the prototype of the species, other breeds bear little resemblance to their forefather. You certainly wouldn't automatically assume that the Miniature Poodle and the Old English Sheepdog have common ancestors.

Broadly speaking, there are seven main groups of dogs. Descriptions of each follow, along with a list of the main breeds within each group.

GUNDOGS OR SPORTING DOGS

A large number of dog breeds evolved according to the jobs humans needed them to do. When the invention of the gun provided a new way of hunting, new varieties of dogs were bred to perform very specific tasks. Dogs with sensitive noses were bred to locate or 'point' to the hunters' targets. Other breeds were developed to flush out or 'spring' the prey, usually birds. Yet more dogs were bred to retrieve the prey once it had been shot. Specific traits were bred into each of these dogs. Retrieving dogs, for instance, were bred to have 'soft mouths', which ensured there was no damage to the birds they recovered.

Common breeds within this category include the Golden Retriever; German Shorthaired Pointer; the Irish, Gordon and English Setters; the Cocker, American Cocker, English Springer and Field Spaniels; and the Labrador and Chesapeake Bay Retrievers. The group also includes the Weimaraner and the Hungarian Vizsla.

WORKING DOGS

Over the centuries, humans have bred dogs to do a huge range of different jobs. Breeds have been produced specifically to rescue people from drowning, guide them across snow-covered mountains, alert them to intruders, sniff out explosives and guide the blind. This diverse collection of working dogs includes the Alaskan Malamute and the Bernese Mountain Dog, the St Bernard and the Dobermann, the Boxer and the Bullmastiff. Each of these was bred to excel at specific activities.

HOUNDS

Some of the earliest breeds developed by man were used as 'sight' or 'gaze' hounds. Such dogs are described in ancient Persian manuscripts and appear in Egyptian tomb paintings. Their special skill was to hunt down prey that humans and their horses, bows and arrows couldn't reach in open country. Often helped by trained falcons, these dogs had the ability to creep up swiftly and silently, running down the prey so that the hunters could close in for the kill. The Saluki and the Afghan are amongst the oldest examples of this group of dog. More modern versions include the Irish Wolfhound and the Greyhound. Centuries later, Europeans developed 'scent' hound breeds that were able to trail quarry over long distances, eventually exhausting it. Some killed the prey, others kept it cornered while baying to attract the hunters to them. The Elkhound was a typical example of this type of dog. More modern versions include the Bloodhound and the Basset Hound.

It is a measure of the diversity of the demands humans have placed on their dogs that this group contains some of the greatest contrasts within the canine world: from the tallest of breeds, the Irish Wolfhound, to one of the shortest, the Dachshund; from the fastest, the Greyhound, to the most silent, the only non-barking breed, the Basenji.

TERRIERS

The name Terrier comes from the Latin *terra*, meaning earth. As the name suggests, the original terriers were bred to hunt creatures considered by humans as vermin that lived both above and below the ground, such as foxes, badgers, rats and otters. Terriers date back many centuries and are believed to have originated largely in Britain. Popular breeds include the Airedale and the Bull, the Cairn and the Fox, the Irish and the West Highland.

TOY DOGS

Dogs haven't only been bred for working purposes, however. Throughout history, man has produced dogs that have provided him with nothing more than warmth and companionship, affection and aesthetic pleasure. Lapdogs, for instance, were – as their name suggests – bred specifically to sit on the laps of Tibetan monks. Elsewhere, aristocrats produced breeds that appealed only for the admiring looks they won in and around the royal court. Toy breeds include the Maltese and the Pomeranian, the Pekingese and the Cavalier King Charles Spaniel, the Yorkshire Terrier and the Bichon Frise.

UTILITY OR NON-SPORTING DOGS

Such is the range of breeds man has created, there are many that don't fit conveniently into any of the main categories in terms of sport or work. Unsurprisingly, the dogs within this group have hugely contrasting appearances. They include such diverse dogs as the Japanese Akita and the Miniature Poodle, the Dalmatian and the Chow Chow, the Mexican Hairless and the Lhasa Apso.

PASTORAL OR HERDING DOGS

Among the most useful and intelligent dogs ever bred are those traditionally used for herding. They have been bred to work in different climates and with different animals, from cattle and sheep to reindeer. Because they work in the face of the elements, they have evolved tough, weatherproofed double coats to protect them from even the most severe weather conditions. The most popular breeds of this type are the German Shepherd and the Border Collie, the Old English Sheepdog and the Samoyed. In different parts of the world, breeds range from the Australian Shepherd and Cattle Dogs to the Belgian Shepherd Dog, from the Finnish Lapphund to the Norwegian Buhund, from the Polish Lowland Sheepdog to the Pyrenean Mountain Dog.

THE WOLF IN YOUR PUPPY

Given their physical differences and the very different environments into which they will be introduced, modern dogs live lives more diverse than those of any other species on earth. Some will work, whether as sheepdogs or guide dogs, sniffer dogs or police dogs, some will breed and raise families, while others will simply provide companionship and pleasure. Whatever breed they are – and whatever life they lead – two things are certain. They all share the same DNA and the same basic programming as their ancient ancestor, the wolf. And because of this each of their lives will conform to a distinct pattern.

It may not seem as though your adorable ball of fluff is a wild animal as it curls itself up in front of your fireplace but, deep within its DNA, that's precisely what it is. You can take the dog out of the wolf pack, but you can't take the wolf pack out of the dog. To understand what your puppy is going through during its first six months, you first need to understand what happens in the natural world.

A wolf pup spends the first part of its life, around six months, in close proximity to the den where it is raised. During these months it passes through the first distinct phases of its life.

For the first three weeks or so, the wolf pup is utterly dependent on its mother. It remains close to her at all times, suckling from her bosom in the den. During this time, the family unit remains undisturbed by the rest of the pack. Despite being the leader of the pack, even their father, the alpha male, stays away during this time.

After three weeks or so, the puppies will be able to walk and make their first, furtive movements away from their mother. At the same time their father, the alpha, and the rest of the pack begin interacting with them. A wolf pack is a well-oiled machine, a tightly knit team in which each member knows its place and its job. And from the very beginning each wolf is groomed to take its position in that chain of command.

During the pups' first weeks every adult wolf has become 'broody', producing a hormone called prolactin. They know the newcomers represent the pack's future survival. They know too that more than half of the new litter will not survive into adulthood. Disease, starvation and predators claim 60 per cent of young wolves before they reach the age of two. So as the pups emerge into the den, the pack begins the job of educating their new members about the day-to-day realities of surviving lupine life.

The messages the pups receive during this phase are powerful and formative ones. They see how facial expression and body language convey important signals about status. They learn how their elders use these signals to avoid confrontations. They see that rank is determined by a combination of experience and personality, with the stronger characters rising to the top of the pack. And by watching the way the grown-up wolves interact, particularly with the alpha male, the pups get their first glimpses of how the very top of that hierarchy works.

But the most immediate lessons they learn come from play. As they begin chasing, retrieving and play-fighting with their siblings, they develop their physical abilities and begin to see where their strengths – and ultimately their place in the pack – lie. This is the very beginning of their preparation for fully-fledged membership of the pack. In time the natural herders, stalkers and attackers will emerge.

By the time it is eight weeks or so old, a wolf pup will be ready to venture a little further afield. It will begin to chase insects, birds or other creatures that gather around the pack. The play rituals it undergoes with its siblings and other members of the pack will intensify. The young wolf will develop its abilities to run and jump, wrestle and bite, skills that it will come to need when it joins the hunters. Any ideas a young wolf might have of heading off on the hunt will be quickly dispelled, however. Leaving the den at this stage would make it vulnerable to attack by predators. The senior wolves will give pups a signal, delivered in clear, unequivocal terms: 'Stay at home; you're not ready to join us yet.' They will also choose one senior wolf to remain with the pups. Once again, the hierarchy of the pack – and the young wolf's place within that structure – is driven home.

By the time it reaches its fifth and sixth months, the wolf pup is developing fast both physically and mentally. Inside the den and around its perimeter, the building blocks are continuing to be laid for its emergence – eighteen months or so down the line – as a mature, adult wolf.

It may seem hard to equate the life of a wild animal to that of the lovable creature that shares your life but it is crucial that you do. The stages of their development are very similar, as are their capabilities at each age. Certain wolf instincts are hard-wired into the brains of domestic dogs, and it is only by seeing your pet as a domesticated wolf that you will be able to understand its behaviour and learn how to deal with it effectively.

In this book, I'll explain all about looking after dogs from birth up to six months, and show the ways in which your puppy's ancestors continue to affect it today.

2 | YOUR PUPPY'S FIRST WEEKS OF LIFE

Most people will acquire a puppy some time after it is eight weeks old. For you to understand your puppy properly, it is important that you understand what goes on during those first eight weeks. How has it developed? What have been the most important moments so far? What factors do you need to bear in mind as you take over ownership of a puppy?

THE EARLY HOURS – BIRTH AND BEYOND

The first few moments of a dog's life are traumatic. The newborn puppy emerges from the warm, safe, dark environment that is the womb into a world filled with new smells and sensations.

Fortunately its mother will be there to reassure and care for it. She will be fixated on its welfare for the crucial first two to three weeks to come.

Because it can't hear or see, the newborn puppy has very little concept of what is happening during the first ten days. It does not yet have any concept of its self or its siblings. It can do little more than sleep, drag itself on to its mother's teat when it feels the need for food and whine when it is feeling cold, hungry or in pain.

The mother's role is all-encompassing during this phase. As well as feeding her pups, she also stimulates them to defecate and urinate then eats their faeces and licks up the urine so as to keep the den clean and free from germs. Not only is she the sole source of food but she is also the only means of keeping warm. A newborn pup can't generate or retain heat so contact with its mother is vital for its survival. This is why the mother hardly strays more than a couple of feet from her newborns during this phase of their young lives.

Yet even at this point, the first signs of personality and status are emerging within the litter. The mother's teats are arranged in pairs along the length of her belly, with the best supply of milk available from the middle teats. Already the litter will have begun jostling for access to these prime feeding stations. Some will have forced themselves on to the best teats, while others will have been forced to feed off the less available outer and forward teats. Some may even have been pushed away from the teats altogether and it's possible they might die.

TEN DAYS TO THREE WEEKS OLD

The first major turning point in a dog's development comes at about ten days. Around this time the eyes begin to open, ungluing themselves from the inside to the out over a period of three to four days. They then learn to focus. At the same time their hearing is beginning to come into operation as well.

With these senses functioning, puppies become aware of the environment around them. Although they spend a huge proportion of their time sleeping they are also noticing – to their surprise – that they are not alone: they have siblings. They learn to recognise their mum by look and by sound as well as by smell. They start sniffing the perimeter of the whelping box as if signalling their readiness to explore the wider world. They will begin getting up on their legs, trying to find their balance and co-ordination and make their first tentative steps. There is a lot of investigation of what they are capable of – and what others are capable of. The puppies will begin climbing over each other, trying to gain height advantage over their siblings. There is a lot of sparring and blatting at this point. There are practical lessons to learn too. At this time, for instance, they learn to lap water from a bowl.

All this activity comes in short bursts, however. Within a maximum of five minutes they will be asleep again.

THREE TO EIGHT WEEKS

By the three-week point in puppies' development, with their eyes, ears and nose all now functioning, they are reacting more to sight, smell and sound. They start to bark and make more sounds. They start to wag their tails. They start scratching themselves and shaking their heads. And they start play fighting with their siblings. This is an extension of the interaction that's been going on already, as they bite each other and try to climb up to give themselves a height advantage. They are developing answers to some key questions. Where do I fit into this pack? What am I capable of doing physically? But they are also asking the question, what

– and who – is outside the immediate confines of the whelping box. They are ready to claim a little independence for themselves.

In the wild, it is now that the pack really comes into its own. While the pups were being suckled by their mother, the alpha female, the excitement has been building in the rest of the pack. The other wolves – both male and female – have been producing prolactin, which makes them 'broody' too. Now, as the mother invites the father and the rest of the extended family to join her, they start to perform their role as surrogate parents.

Wolves from all parts of the pack hierarchy will do their bit to educate, assimilate and act as mentors for the new pup. This is how the pup gains the important information it will need in order to be a properly functioning – and happy – adult member of the pack. They will set boundaries – gently dragging the pups back when they wander too far from the den. In short, they are teaching them the rules and the language of the pack.

A domestic dog is living in a very different social organisation – but it is still vital that the dog begins to get the information it will need to function within that organisation. And it is vital that that knowledge is imparted now, when its most important imprinting is happening. It is up to us, as humans, to perform the same role as the pack that would be its teachers in the wild.

HANDLING PUPPIES

It is around three weeks old that breeders should start handling puppies, getting them used to the sight, smells and sounds of humans. This is vitally important for the rest of the puppy's development so from the outset the aim is for the puppy to associate human contact with warmth, comfort and above all safety. While a little stress is good for the dog's development – making it ask 'What happens now?' – too much stress has to be avoided at all costs.

To pick up a puppy, follow these steps:

1. Crouch down to ground level.
2. Place your hands underneath the puppy and scoop it up gently but confidently.
3. Remaining in the crouched position, raise it up off the ground to eye level.
4. Reward the puppy by placing it in your arms, stroking it gently and making calm, reassuring noises.

If this is done correctly, the puppy will make the association that you are a safe zone. When it feels unsafe in the future and begins to ask questions about where it should go, you will already have provided one potential answer.

This is why you should never pick up a puppy by the scruff of its neck, as some people advocate. This habit is based on a misconception by humans who have seen dogs picking up their young with their teeth. They miss two important points: firstly, the dog clamps its teeth on the pup's back area, not on the neck; and secondly, it only does so because it doesn't have hands to do the job. If it did, it wouldn't be using its teeth. We do have hands and we should use them. By picking the puppy up by the scruff of its neck, you are inflicting pain on it. This creates a totally negative association, which will be a barrier to you bonding with the dog in the days and weeks to come.

Carers who don't interact with their puppies during this crucial phase of their development are losing valuable time. Indeed, there is strong scientific evidence that a puppy's instinct to investigate and socialise is at its peak during this early five-week period, after which it begins to fall away. Dogs who haven't been exposed to humans and their environment by the age of 14 weeks find it problematical to do so in later life.

Go through this picking-up process twice a day from the age of three weeks onwards. As the puppy gets to trust you more you can extend and develop this interaction. This will allow you to pave the way for its interaction with other humans, vets in particular.

1. Place the puppy on a raised surface, like a table. Make sure it is covered and stable, as sudden movement will frighten them.
2. Begin a little bit of grooming, running a very soft brush through its coat.
3. Begin placing your fingers in its mouth, so as to open the jaw and inspect the mouth.
4. Begin holding its head so as to inspect its ears.
5. Teach the puppy to roll on its side in a submissive position. This will achieve two things: preparing the

dog for future visits to the vet and also underlining the dominance it has already begun to associate with you.

6. Get the puppy used to you touching its feet. A lot of dogs don't like having their feet touched, so it's a huge benefit to get over this hurdle early on. This is best done when the puppy is tired so it is easier to work with.

TEACHING RECOGNITION OF ITS NAME

The most important thing you want to instil in your dog during this first eight weeks is the belief that there is nothing threatening in a human voice. When you or anyone else speaks, you want the dog to associate the sound with all things warm and positive. It is too soon to start teaching it specific commands, such as 'sit' or 'come', but the puppy will soon have to learn some discipline and self-control. For now it is important that it delights in your company and that it makes a positive association with your voice.

There is one important thing you can do at the moment, and that is to get the puppy to recognise its own name. In doing this you are laying in place some important groundwork for when you get down to training it properly.

The first thing you need to do is choose a name. Once the puppy's name has been chosen it's a good idea to use it from the very first time you are picking it up and showing it affection at around three weeks of age. It will be possible to change the dog's name when it moves home, but if it is destined for another home and you know the likely owner, it is helpful if they choose the name you start working with from an early stage.

The next thing to do is start addressing the puppy within its litter, using that name. At this point the dog doesn't see itself as an individual so much as a litter member, so it is possible it may not respond immediately. But if it does, your goal is to get it to stop, look at you and – for the first time – ask 'Are you talking to me?'

There are a few key points to remember when doing this.

- 🐾 Eye contact is crucial. When you call one of the puppies they may all look at you but you must only look at the individual you are addressing.
- 🐾 Make sure your eyes are soft and inviting; don't glare or look anxious.
- 🐾 When you call the name, do so in a happy way; the tone should be soft, as should the body language.
- 🐾 If the dog comes to you on its own, praise it warmly, repeating the name.
- 🐾 If the whole litter comes, make a point of only praising the one dog; you are also trying to teach the pups that it is not their name, and this will help reinforce that message.

The beauty of this is that it is something you can build on. When you are teaching the dog to make a positive association with something during weaning or toilet training, for instance, repeating the name warmly as you reward it will help.

All this should have a drip effect on the dog. It should soon recognise the distinctive sound of its own name, providing you – and its future owners – with a foundation on which to work.

WEANING

Between three and five weeks of age, the puppy is ready to be weaned off its mother's milk.

In the wild, this is the point at which the alpha female will relinquish her duties as the sole provider of sustenance and take a back seat to the rest of the pack. A mother of domestic puppies behaves in this same instinctive way, standing up to feed rather than lying down, thereby allowing herself to move away if she feels she has finished or if she is being hurt by the puppy's pin-sharp baby teeth or claws.

It will take the puppy around three weeks to make the transition off its mother's teat. During that time it may still suckle and feed, but as the demands of her puppies slowly decrease, the female's milk will dry up so owners will notice that feeding times shorten in length. During the early stages of weaning the puppy's diet may be divided 50–50 between its mother's milk and other food, but by the end of the sixth week a puppy should be eating independently of its mother.

Many people begin weaning with a cereal, such as porridge mixed with milk. Some opt for tinned puppy food. Others go for kibbles of 'complete food' made up of carefully selected ingredients that constitute an ideal diet. Many people opt for raw meat.

The puppy will by now have a full complement of teeth coming through, but their jaws are still too weak for it to crunch anything and its throat is still too narrow to swallow food of any size. It is vital that whatever food you choose to introduce, it is of the right consistency. Porridge with milk should be as smooth as possible, while kibbles should be soaked in cold water overnight then mixed in a food processor for better consistency. Tinned food must also be softened so that it is palatable for the puppy. If you go for the raw-meat option, make sure it is minced well.

Follow these instructions for the first feed.

1. Pick up the puppy gently, speaking to it softly. Don't make any sudden movements.
2. Pinch together your thumb and third and fourth fingers. Scoop the food onto your fingers, then put it under the puppy's nose for a moment or two so it can smell it.
3. How quickly it accepts the food depends on personality. Some will only need to smell it and they will be digging in, while others will be cautious and unsure. If they are enthusiastic, be careful they don't bite. If they are reluctant, be patient.
4. When the puppy has eaten, stroke it softly with one finger and give it some gentle words of praise.

This is the first time the puppy will have associated you with the providing of food. It is vital that you make it a good association by taking things slowly and doing all you can to make it as pleasant an experience as possible. Time spent getting this right can make the difference between a relationship that works and one that doesn't. Don't rush it.

TOILETTING

Until now, as we have seen, the mother both stimulates defecation and cleans up afterwards. This is no longer the case. By the start of the third week, the puppy will have begun to make its first moves away from the whelping box. Generally the front of the box is removed around this time, allowing them to move a few feet away from their sleeping area towards the boundary of the den.

They will begin to defecate and urinate on their own. This new independence coincides with the mother's gradual removal of herself from the scene.

A puppy of three to four weeks will urinate 12 or more times a day and will open its bowels five to six times a day.

At first the puppy will probably do its toiletting around the den. Dogs are by nature clean creatures so the puppy will try to put as much distance as it can between its sleeping and feeding area and its toilet area. You must ensure you have something in place for puppies to go to the toilet on. There are plenty of alternatives: newspapers or absorbent padding or perhaps wood shavings (make sure they are dust-free).

The puppy isn't going to get to this area every time, of course, so during this phase it is vital you keep the bedding area immaculately clean. You can buy absorbent bedding that takes wetness through to the bottom. A lining of newspaper between this and the floor will provide another layer to take up moisture. This should be changed as often as need be, perhaps even two or three times a day during the early stage of toilet training.

Dogs prefer to do their toiletting in a natural environment so it is good for both you and your dog if you progress the training to a garden or outdoor area as soon as possible. You should start doing this at about four weeks of age. They should have got the hang of walking by then.

- 🐾 Accompany the dog to the toilet first thing in the morning, after meals and when it wakes from a sleep.
- 🐾 Stay with it in the garden or outdoor area. When you see it squatting, give it a food reward and use a word such as 'empty' or 'clean dog'.

There are going to be occasions when it catches you out, so be careful to line the dog's route from the sleeping area to the garden with whatever it is you are using to absorb the mess. The ideal thing would be a flap leading straight from the den to the garden.

If the puppy has accidents away from the toilet area, the important thing is not to chastise it. Clear it up without a word. The key to toilet training is making it a good association, so anything negative at this stage is unhelpful. With a positive association being built all the time, it won't take the puppy long to make the connection between wanting to go to the toilet and going outside.

🐾 🐾 🐾 🐾 🐾 🐾 🐾

By eight weeks of age, the puppy will be ready to move on to a new home without its mother and siblings. The better the care it has received in these early weeks, the more easily it will cope with the trauma of the change of environment. In the next chapter, you'll find advice for new owners on choosing a puppy at this stage.

3 | CHOOSING YOUR DOG

Before looking at the details of how to introduce a puppy into your home, it is important to discuss how you acquire a new dog. To my mind, there are only two sources from which we should buy dogs: respectable, responsible breeders and registered rescue centres or dogs' homes.

There is, I know, a wide range of alternative sources – from pet shops and so-called licensed kennels, classified ads or even from a chance encounter with a seller in a pub or at a fairground.

The problem with buying from a stranger is obvious, in that you will have no comeback if anything goes wrong. A friend of mine once saw a batch of dogs for sale at a horse fair. There were no clues as to where these dogs had come from. Their owners had only one interest: making money. My friend was a soft touch and took pity on one dog in particular. During the next two years she spent more than £2,500 on vets bills, because it turned out the dog was riddled with worms and suffered from a variety of stomach problems. The crucial point here is that she had no way of seeking compensation from the people who sold her that dog. She didn't even get a contact name.

This type of trade is sadly on the increase. The growth of so-called puppy farms, where dogs are bred in a factory-style environment, is something I abhor. Here in the UK the vast majority of pet dealers and licensed kennels are supplied by puppy farms, and owners who buy from them will often be allowed no more than 48 hours in which to return their dogs. How on earth is anyone supposed to decide whether they will be able to share their life with a dog in that space of time? Health problems may not have emerged within that period, and the dog's true personality might be masked beneath its anxiety about the new surroundings.

It is my firm belief that if at all possible an owner should be able to meet – at least – the puppy's mother before taking the dog away. This is something I will explain in more detail in a moment. You should be able to visit the breeder and see the puppy interacting with its mother and siblings. Be suspicious if you can't; in puppy farms, mother and pups are separated early on. The absence of the mother may mean that the seller is a third party, whose motives are purely to do with money rather than the welfare of the dogs in their protection.

No reputable breeder or rescue centre would sell a dog without guaranteeing that the owner could return the animal to them if they were unable to keep the dog for whatever reason. The dog cannot lose under this arrangement. If it fits into a happy home it will enjoy a long and hopefully rewarding life there. If not, it will return to a place where its best interests are safeguarded.

Owners who leave themselves with no comeback are not able to return an unwanted dog. Many will, of course, ensure they are given good homes but, sadly, many more will not. And that is something I cannot condone.

BUYING A PUPPY

Falling in love with a puppy is the easiest thing in the world. We've all experienced the aaaaaaah factor, that moment when we've stared for the first time into the saucer-sized eyes of a cute young dog and gone hopelessly gooey. It's for this reason that I recommend people begin their search for a puppy by steering clear of these charmers to begin with.

We know that owners are going to fall head over heels in love with the puppy. It's a given. Far better for them to deal with the realities before beginning the romance. And the best way to do this is by first meeting the parents.

Producing a litter of puppies involves a collaboration between the human breeder and the dogs. The dogs deliver this new life into the world, but it is the former who must shoulder the ultimate responsibility. I passionately believe that the best way to assess whether a dog is coming from a good home is by getting to know both sets of 'parents' – human and canine.

Given that many breeders go to stud to begin their litters, it is more than likely that only the mother will be available. Her personality, temperament and general demeanour will reveal much. If you are able to meet the father as well, this will provide the clearest possible idea of the sort of dog its offspring is going to become.

Just as importantly, the attitude of the breeder is highly revealing. Is their home well-kept? How does the breeder behave towards the dogs? The extent to which the breeder interrogates all potential new owners is a good indication of the quality of the home. You should expect to be grilled by a good breeder. Personally, I insist on knowing as much as I can about anyone who wants to take one of my puppies into their home. It's like an adoption society; reputable breeders – and registered rescue centres – are very careful about where they place the 'children' entrusted to their care. A good breeder is responsible for innocent young lives and they should want to know everything about the home into which they are considering releasing the puppy. They should always ask what the domestic situation is at home.

- 🐾 Are there people around all day to look after the dog?
- 🐾 Are there many small children in the home?
- 🐾 Have they owned this type of dog – or indeed any dog – before?
- 🐾 Have the prospective owners thought about whether the particular breed is right for their home?

The fact that the breeder, or rescue centre, asks these questions should be seen as a positive sign. If they are not asking these questions, they are probably more interested in making a sale than the dog's welfare and should, therefore, be treated with caution.

By the same token, a good breeder should be open to questions from a potential owner. They should be willing to reveal anything and everything about the dog's history and background – from the details of its parentage and its age, to its favourite food and toys. I've suggested a list of questions to ask below. Again, owners should be wary of anyone who is vague or unhappy about answering these questions.

Questions to ask a breeder or rescue centre

- What is the dog's background?
- Who are its parents (if known)? Can you meet them?
- What age is the dog?
- Favourite foods?
- At what times is it fed, and what quantities of food?
- Favourite toys?
- What medical checks has it had?
- Has it been wormed?
- Has it had any vaccinations?
- Has it had its eye test to check for inherited conditions?
- Have any health problems been identified?
- Are there any procedures required by the breed standard, such as removal of a dew claw? If so, have they been done?
- Do its parents suffer from any hereditary problems that could have been passed on?
- Can you have the breed certification documents?

Potential owners should be particularly careful about checking for hereditary problems within some breeds. Cavalier King Charles Spaniels are prone to heart problems, for instance. Long-backed breeds like Basset Hounds and

Dachshunds have a tendency to suffer from back pain and slipped discs. In German Shepherds and Labradors, potential buyers should look out for hip dysplasia, a genetic problem in which the ball and socket joint of the hip can be deformed or even non-existent. It is a condition that is extremely painful and ultimately crippling for dogs that are afflicted and something that good breeders monitor closely. Dogs are routinely x-rayed at the age of one and given a 'hip score' – which ranges from zero for perfect hips to 18 and higher, a mark which indicates the dog should not be used for breeding. Signs of hip dysplasia can manifest themselves even earlier than this, so it is wise to observe puppies for any tell-tale signs of discomfort in walking, such as 'hopping' when they walk.

So as to make informed and appropriate choices, potential owners are advised to research the breeds they are interested in. This is easily done through the Kennel Club or its equivalent organisation overseas and after that the various breed experts. The importance of this cannot be over-stressed. No one goes out to make a major purchase such as a new car or a house without researching the subject thoroughly. When they choose a dog, owners are introducing into the family a new member that will hopefully remain with them for 12 to 14 years. It is not something to be taken lightly.

BREEDS APART: WHAT DIFFERENT DOGS DEMAND FROM THEIR OWNERS

Hundreds of years of selective breeding by humans has produced a bewildering array of different dogs. And, for all their essential similarities, these dogs bring with them their own set of special needs. Some will need more exercise than others. Some will need much more grooming. Others will have a significantly shorter lifespan and will, therefore, incur the inevitable medical costs associated with old age that much sooner. Size is a factor too. The giant breeds need enough space in which to move and grow. Anyone considering acquiring a dog should take all these factors into consideration.

The demands of the different breeds fall into the following broad categories.

PHYSICAL DEMANDS

Some dogs have been bred to be more athletic and energetic than others. Gundogs or sporting dogs, for instance, will tend to demand a lot of exercise. These Springers, Pointers and Setters were, after all, bred to work on the hunt and are able to run for long periods during a normal hunting day. They also tend to love water and may be drawn to retrieve or chase birds, because of generations of breeding. Similarly, pastoral or herding breeds tend to be attracted to other species of animals and may instinctively try to herd them. Not every owner is going to have a flock of sheep for their Collie or German Shepherd to round up, but they should be prepared to give these dogs a proper outlet for their considerable energies. They need homes that are going to be up to the challenge of giving them plenty of exercise and play time.

At the other end of the scale, the toy dog group includes many breeds that were designed to provide little more than companionship and warmth, sometimes literally. Toy breeds such as the Chihuahua, Pekingese, Pomeranian and Maltese don't need huge amounts of exercise.

SPATIAL DEMANDS

The size of a dog is a factor that needs to be taken into consideration. While toy dogs will not take up much space, large working dogs will fill almost any space they occupy. If they are active dogs as well, this could cause owners problems in a small or restrictive space. Everyone, of course, has the right to own the breed of their choice, but allowances should be made for the living space they require.

GROOMING DEMANDS

Dogs are naturally clean animals, and take a great deal of care of their condition. As a result, some breeds require next to no grooming. Smooth-coated dogs such as the Labrador Retriever or the Great Dane, for instance, are low maintenance compared to other breeds. By contrast, there are some breeds that have been bred purely for their look and consequently have exceedingly long, high-maintenance coats. Breeds that spring to mind here include Afghan Hounds, Spaniels, Old English Sheepdogs, the Bichon Frise and Poodle breeds. Dogs in the Terrier group can also require 'hand stripping' (see page 32) to keep their coats looking good.

DOGS WITH MEDICAL/LIFESPAN DEMANDS
The average life expectancy of different breeds varies enormously. Working breeds tend to be bigger dogs so they usually live shorter lives. Smaller toy dogs, on the other hand, tend to live to more advanced ages. Dogs with shorter lifespans are going to need medical care earlier than those with longer lifespans. Old age tends to be the period when the most visits to the vet are required. If the dog isn't going to live much beyond seven years then, inevitably, this period is going to arrive sooner than if they live to 15 or beyond. They need owners who are willing to meet this challenge.

DIFFERENT BREEDS, DIFFERENT DEMANDS
The tables on the following pages illustrate the different demands of dogs within each of the seven main groups.

KEY

SIZE
S   Small
M   Medium
L   Large
X   Extra large

GROOMING AND EXERCISE
L   Little needed
M   Moderate needed
C   Considerable needed

LIFESPAN
A   under 9 years on average
B   9–15 years on average
C   over 15 years on average

DIFFERENT BREEDS – DIFFERENT DEMANDS
THE DIFFERENT REQUIREMENTS OF THE
MOST POPULAR BREEDS

TYPE OF DOG	SIZE	GROOMING	EXERCISE	LIFESPAN
GUNDOGS/SPORTING				
English Setter	L	M	C	B
German Longhaired Pointer	L	M	C	B
German Shorthaired Pointer	L	L	C	B
German Wirehaired Pointer	L	M	C	B
Gordon Setter	L	M	C	B
Hungarian Vizsla	L	L	C	B
Irish Red & White Setter	L	M	C	B
Irish Setter	L	M	C	B
Pointer	L	L	C	B
Retriever (Chesapeake Bay)	L	M	C	B
Retriever (Curly Coated)	L	M	C	B
Retriever (Flat Coated)	L	M	C	B
Retriever (Golden)	L	M	C	B
Retriever (Labrador)	L	L	C	B
Spaniel (American Cocker)	M	C	M	B
Spaniel (Cocker)	M	C	M	B
Spaniel (English Springer)	M	M	C	B
Spaniel (Field)	M	M	C	B
Spaniel (Irish Water)	M	M	C	B
Spaniel (Sussex)	M	M	C	B

TYPE OF DOG	SIZE	GROOMING	EXERCISE	LIFESPAN
Spaniel (Welsh Springer)	M	M	C	B
Spanish Water Dog	M	M	M	B
Weimaraner	L	L	C	B

WORKING

	SIZE	GROOMING	EXERCISE	LIFESPAN
Alaskan Malamute	L	C	C	B
Bernese Mountain Dog	X	M	M	A
Bouvier Des Flandres	L	C	C	B
Boxer	L	L	C	B
Bullmastiff	L	L	C	B
Canadian Eskimo Dog	L	M	C	B
Doberman	L	L	C	B
German Pinscher	M	L	M	B
Giant Schnauzer	L	C	C	B
Great Dane	X	L	C	A
Mastiff	X	L	M	A
Newfoundland	X	C	C	B
Rottweiler	L	L	C	B
St Bernard	X	C	M	A
Siberian Husky	L	M	C	B

TERRIER

	SIZE	GROOMING	EXERCISE	LIFESPAN
Airedale	L	C	M	B
Australian	S	M	M	B
Bedlington	M	M	M	B

TYPE OF DOG	SIZE	GROOMING	EXERCISE	LIFESPAN
Border	S	M	M	B
Bull	M	L	M	B
Bull (Miniature)	M	L	M	B
Cairn	S	M	M	B
Fox (Smooth)	M	L	M	B
Fox (Wire)	M	C	M	B
Irish	M	M	M	B
Kerry Blue	M	C	M	B
Lakeland	M	C	M	B
Norfolk	S	M	M	B
Parson Russell	M	L	M	B
Scottish	M	C	M	B
Skye	M	M	M	B
Staffordshire Bull	M	L	C	B
Welsh	M	C	M	B
West Highland White	S	C	M	B

HOUNDS

Afghan	L	C	C	B
Basenji	M	L	M	B
Basset Hound	M	L	C	B
Beagle	M	L	C	B
Bloodhound	L	L	C	A
Borzoi	L	M	C	B
Dachshund (Long or Wire Haired)	M	M	M	B

TYPE OF DOG	SIZE	GROOMING	EXERCISE	LIFESPAN
Dachshund (Miniature Long or Wire Haired)	S	M	M	C
Dachshund (Smooth Haired)	M	L	M	B
Dachshund (Miniature Smooth Haired)	S	L	M	C
Norwegian Elkhound	L	M	C	B
Foxhound	L	L	C	B
Greyhound	L	L	M	B
Irish Wolfhound	X	M	C	A
Pharaoh Hound	L	L	C	B
Rhodesian Ridgeback	L	L	C	B
Saluki	L	M	C	B
Whippet	M	L	C	B

PASTORAL/HERDING

	SIZE	GROOMING	EXERCISE	LIFESPAN
Anatolian Shepherd	L	M	C	B
Australian Cattle	M	L	M	B
Australian Shepherd	L	M	C	B
Bearded Collie	L	C	M	B
Border Collie	M	M	C	B
Collie (Rough)	L	C	C	B
Collie (Smooth)	L	L	C	B
German Shepherd	L	M	C	B
Old English Sheepdog	L	C	C	B
Pyrenean Mountain Dog	X	C	M	A
Pyrenean Sheepdog	M	M	M	B
Samoyed	L	C	C	B

TYPE OF DOG	SIZE	GROOMING	EXERCISE	LIFESPAN
Shetland Sheepdog	M	C	M	B
Welsh Corgi (Cardigan)	M	L	M	B
Welsh Corgi (Pembroke)	M	L	M	B

TOYS

	SIZE	GROOMING	EXERCISE	LIFESPAN
Affen Pinscher	S	M	L	B
Australian Silky Terrier	S	M	L	B
Bichon Frise	S	C	L	B
Cavalier King Charles Spaniel	S	M	M	B
Chihuahua (Long Coat)	S	M	L	B
Chihuahua (Smooth Coat)	S	L	L	B
English Toy Terrier (Black and Tan)	S	L	L	B
Maltese	S	C	L	B
Miniature Pinscher	S	L	L	B
Papillon	S	M	L	B
Pekingese	S	C	L	B
Pomeranian	S	C	L	B
Pug	S	L	L	B
Yorkshire Terrier	S	C	L	B

UTILITY

	SIZE	GROOMING	EXERCISE	LIFESPAN
Akita	L	M	C	B
Boston Terrier	S	L	M	B
Bulldog	M	L	M	A
Chow Chow	L	C	M	B

TYPE OF DOG	SIZE	GROOMING	EXERCISE	LIFESPAN
Dalmatian	L	L	C	B
French Bulldog	S	L	M	B
German Spitz (Klein)	S	C	L	B
German Spitz (Mittel)	M	C	L	B
Japanese Shiba Inu	M	M	M	B
Japanese Spitz	M	C	M	B
Lhasa Apso	S	C	L	B
Mexican Hairless	M	L	M	B
Miniature Schnauzer	S	C	M	B
Poodle (Miniature)	M	C	M	C
Poodle (Standard)	L	C	C	C
Poodle (Toy)	S	C	M	C
Schnauzer	M	C	M	B
Shar Pei	M	L	M	B
Shih Tzu	S	C	M	B
Tibetan Spaniel	S	M	M	C
Tibetan Terrier	M	C	M	B

CHOOSING A PUPPY

You've selected the breed of dog you want, you've found a good breeder or rescue centre, and now it's time to pick the individual puppy you will take home with you. A good breeder will be able to brief you on the personalities of the puppies in a litter and will try to help you choose a dog that will suit your lifestyle. They don't want to place an extrovert dog with an owner who is looking for a quiet companion; nor do they want to place a very docile, shy dog with someone who intends leading a very active outdoor life with that dog. The consequences of mismatching dogs and their owners can be awful.

Broad personality types are often apparent early on when the litter is first formed. There are the strong characters who dominate the best feeding positions when suckling from the mother's teats, and there are the weaker members who have been knocked away from these positions and literally have to fight for their food – and their survival. But personality is a more complex matter than this and requires a little study. With the first part of their development well under way, the five or six week mark offers the perfect opportunity to conduct a simple personality test that will answer many of your questions.

There are all sorts of theories about how to conduct personality tests on dogs – many of them bordering on the barbaric. For instance, some people advocate pinching the dog to see how it reacts. I can think of nothing worse. The following three simple tests will give you all the information you need, without resorting to violence or cruelty.

TESTING BY EYE

The first clues about character come early on. By watching which puppies get to the teat first you can spot the dominant characters as well as the shy, retiring ones that get pushed to the back of the litter. This continues as the puppies emerge from under their mother's wing. As they begin to play and interact, you may notice that one takes toys from another. Is there one that just sits there and watches while the others play? You can see that this dog is a thinker, one who will always weigh up its options in life before making its move.

There are signals in terms of body language too, with some dogs looking to assert themselves by placing their bodies over pups they consider to be subordinate. Of course, testing by eye isn't going to tell you everything, so there are a couple of physical tests you can try to fill in the picture.

TESTING IN THE PALM OF THE HAND

This is designed to test the puppy's reaction to being lifted. It will, of course, be used to this by now, but the way it reacts each time speaks volumes.

Lift the puppy off the ground. Place it in the palm of one hand (or two hands if it is a larger breed) and leave it there for ten seconds or so.

- 🐾 If it goes limp in your hand, it is likely to be a more relaxed personality.
- 🐾 If it starts to struggle immediately that indicates it is more stubborn and more likely to challenge you. It might also be a sign of a nervous dog.

☙ If it stays there for a little while then starts to struggle, that indicates a dog who thinks about things first before acting.

TESTING BY LYING THE PUPPY ON ITS BACK
This is designed to test the puppy's reaction to being turned on its back. As with the palm of the hand test, it is not something you should do for long – ten seconds at the absolute maximum.

Lift the puppy and carefully cradle it in your arms. Placing a hand on each side, lift it up and turn it so it is lying on its back in your arms. Five distinct personality types will reveal themselves as follows.

The defiant one
Some puppies simply will not have it. The moment you turn them over they will immediately right themselves, and they will repeat the process every time you try. This dog is going to grow into a strong character, an alpha type. It will take strong, firm and clear leadership to keep it on the straight and narrow.

The resistance fighter
This one will fight you at first, but will eventually comply and lie on its back, under protest. This again is a dog that may present a few problems, but one who will respond to the right signals.

The thinker

Some puppies will initially lie down willingly. They will stay there for a couple of seconds then spring back upright. This indicates a dog that has weighed up the situation, come to a decision – that it doesn't like this – and acted upon it. This is a dog that has a lot of courage and intelligence.

The cool customer

Some pups present no resistance whatsoever; they simply go limp and lie there. This is a chilled-out, laid-back individual. With the right guidance, this is going to be a relatively trouble-free dog.

The bundle of nerves

Some puppies will curl up in a ball almost foetally. This is a sure sign of nervousness in the dog. A dog that reacts this way is going to be prone to anxiety attacks when they hear loud noises or are faced with strange situations. In the worst cases, they may develop problems such as wetting themselves. By identifying them as nervous dogs, however, you can factor this personality into your life with the dog and act accordingly, hopefully avoiding problems.

❀ ❀ ❀ ❀ ❀ ❀ ❀ ❀

Choose a dog with a personality type that is going to fit with the lifestyle you want to introduce it to, whether that be noisy city life or a quiet country existence, and you'll have a head start in getting it to adapt to its new home when it gets there.

CANINE COMPANIONSHIP

Dogs share the human's sense of family values. In general, they enjoy company, whether human or canine, in the home. This sociable nature may be rooted in their ancient past, when they were forming the first communities with our ancient ancestors. But it may go deeper than that. Why else would man have chosen the wolf above any other creature to domesticate first? Did they see them as more companionable than any other animal? It is food for thought.

If you already have a dog at home and want to introduce a new one, it should be planned with care. Introducing an eight-week-old dog to an existing pack is a relatively straightforward process, but you might have more difficulty with a slightly older dog. Bringing a nine-month-old puppy into a home is the equivalent of introducing a hyperactive 12-year-old child. Older dogs, in particular, may not take kindly to their peace and quiet being disturbed.

There are other factors to consider too, as dogs can find it hard to read signals from breeds that are physically different from them. While a toy Poodle and an Irish Wolfhound will get along together eventually, there may be a great deal of friction because of the huge differences in their physical make-up before they settle into a routine together. There's more about dogs' abilities to understand each other's signals on pages 172–8.

For all these reasons, it is advisable to introduce the new dog to its prospective pack as soon as possible. It would be ideal if you could take the existing dog or dogs to the breeder from where the eight-week-old puppy is coming and introduce them there. This has several obvious advantages. In territorial terms, it is neutral ground. The new arrival will also be amongst people who know and can control it in the event of problems. Most importantly of all, if after a few meetings there is clearly a high degree of friction between the old and new dogs, the potential owner will have the chance to think again.

There's more on introducing your puppy to any other dogs at home on pages 48–50.

❧ ❧ ❧ ❧ ❧ ❧ ❧

The vast majority of owners take delivery of their puppy around the age of eight weeks. This is the ideal age for it to make the transition from its litter to a new human environment. As we have seen, a good breeder will have begun the process of weaning the puppy on to solid food and also toilet training it. They will have introduced the puppy to human company by handling and playing with it, and it should respond to its own name. It is now up to you to continue the good work.

4 | MAKING YOUR NEW PUPPY FEEL AT HOME

A pup of eight to 12 weeks old is the equivalent of a four-year-old child and, like a four-year-old human, its needs are simple. First and foremost it needs to know that it is secure and safe. The dog will harbour many fears at this stage – of loud noises, strange smells, unfamiliar faces – and it needs to feel that it is going to be protected from the sometimes bewildering influences at work in the outside world. This need will be especially great for pups who are just leaving the litter and joining their new homes and human families.

As it explores the world around it, the puppy needs to be able to understand how this exciting new environment works. It needs to learn where the boundaries lie, and what is and isn't acceptable behaviour. If it has left its mother's side, it also needs to establish a relationship with a new parent or protector figure in the human world. It is up to the owner to fulfil these two crucial roles, but fortunately they complement each other perfectly. By correctly performing the first, the owner is automatically performing the second.

Your dog's personality has been moulded by its first eight weeks within the litter. But, as we know, development is about both nature and nurture. That nurturing has begun in the litter, but as the dog moves into the human world, it gets under way in earnest.

THE YOUNG DOG'S NEEDS

So what does a dog need so that it can be nurtured into a happy, well-adjusted adult? And what questions is it asking now, especially if – as will be the case for the vast majority of eight-week-old dogs – it is arriving in a new, human home.

Practically speaking, it needs places where it can sleep, eat, play and defecate. It then needs a human owner who is going to feed, exercise and show it the way things work within their world. Beyond that, however, the puppy's first priority is to satisfy itself that it is safe, that there is nothing about which it needs to be afraid. As it gets used to its new environment, it is looking for comfort and security.

Once it has satisfied itself that it is safe, the dog will start exploring the boundaries of this new world and trying to understand its place within it, where it can and can't go in safety. So the puppy is asking itself a series of key questions.

- How far can I go physically and behaviourally without endangering myself?
- Who is going to protect me now?
- Who rules the roost in this new, extended pack?
- And where do I stand in the hierarchy of this pack?

In the litter there was no question where the pups' security lay – it was with their mother. In the new home the dog is looking for the structure that will make it feel safe again. At first it has no clue where it is going to find that structure so it must explore and investigate to find that out. In doing so, of course, it will make mistakes.

THE FIRST 48 HOURS

Leaving its mother and siblings is a traumatic experience for an eight-week-old dog. It is stepping into a world populated by another species, a strange and unsettling place where everyone is speaking an unintelligible language and behaving according to a set of rules about which the dog has no concept. On top of this, the place is filled with a host of unfamiliar sights, sounds and smells. It's not hard to see that this would freak out any creature. The most important thing a new owner can do during the first 48 hours or so is to make it as trauma-free as possible.

Some dogs settle into a new home immediately. They are running around like a rocket within seconds of coming in through the door. Others, however, take longer, so you must be prepared for anything.

The settling-in process can begin the moment the dog arrives at the house. The first thing you should do, immediately upon arrival, is take the dog outside to do its toiletting. When the dog relieves itself, reward it with a small piece of meat, or meat-strip. This should be accompanied with warm words of encouragement, such as 'good dog' or 'clean dog', and perhaps a stroke of the head or nape of the neck area. The key point here is that the first piece of positive association has been achieved within the first few moments in the home. A good start has been made.

The next stage is to allow the dog to get to know its new environment. Let it explore those areas it is free to roam in, with the areas where you don't want it to go blocked off (see pages 54–5). Throughout this, you should be giving out gently affectionate signs, smiles and words of reassurance and kindness. At the same time, however, you should not be gushing or over-affectionate with the dog. This will only set a precedent that will be hard to overcome later.

The puppy's first meal in your house should be as similar as possible to the meals it was used to at the breeder's or rescue centre. Moving home is a stressful experience, so anything that provides continuity for the young dog is to be welcomed. Food, of course, is the ultimate comfort so it is important that owners try to keep the dog's diet the same as it was at its previous home, at least until the dog has settled a little.

A reputable breeder should be able to provide a written diet sheet, with details of the type of food the puppy has been used to as well as quantities and feeding times. Even if you don't like the diet, it is advisable to keep the dog on it for a few days. Young dogs arriving in a new home often show signs of stomach upsets and diarrhoea brought on by the trauma of being separated from their mother and entering a strange environment. Radical changes in diets will only exacerbate this.

If and when you do decide to change the diet, only do so once the dog is comfortable in your home. Introduce the changes at a gentle pace, over a period of three to four days if possible – certainly once the stress of the settling-in period has passed. There's advice on what to feed puppies in chapter 5, pages 67–75.

The first night is going to be particularly difficult for the pup. A dark house, with all its odd bumps and creaks, is going to be an unsettling place. For this reason, it is a good idea to let it sleep close to you. Some people go to the extreme of actually having the dog in bed with them. This isn't going to suit everyone, but placing a basket with a warm, soft blanket somewhere near the bed, where the dog can smell, hear and see you, is the best alternative. Leave a water bowl within easy reach of the puppy too. If, on the other hand, you don't want it in your bedroom, spending the night downstairs on the sofa with the puppy close by is another option. This should only happen once – or possibly twice. Don't let the dog grow used to it. During the first 48 hours, however, it is important that you are around and the dog has access to you, to help it feel secure and protected in its new environment.

It can help the puppy to acclimatise if you bring familiar items from the kennel where it has been with its litter. A piece of bedding or cloth from the den can act in the same way as a security blanket works for a child. A favourite toy is another good idea, if the breeder will let you bring it with you. It can help make the transition from the old home to the new one a considerably less stressful experience for the puppy.

INTRODUCING THE PUPPY TO OTHER DOGS IN THE HOUSE

If you have already taken your old dog or dogs to meet the new puppy, then you have a head start. If not, you can prepare the puppy for their first meeting by bringing an item of theirs in the car with you so they can pick up the smell for the first time.

If the existing pack is only going to meet the new dog on the day of its arrival, this introduction must be the first task of the day. Owners must choose a neutral ground – and be careful to avoid places where the existing pack has strong associations. They will need the assistance of another handler, someone to look after either the new dog or the existing pack.

If there is more than one dog in the existing pack, owners should introduce each dog to the newcomer one at a time. The key thing here is that each time this happens, the two dogs must meet on equal status. As the newcomer is going to be on a lead, the existing pack member should also be on a lead. If one is being rewarded with toys or treats, then so should the other. This has the added benefit of reinforcing your own primacy within the pack.

The dogs should then be allowed to get to know each other while still being kept on the lead a few feet apart. The important thing here is not to panic. They will size each other up, but if they begin to grumble or growl at each other don't be overly concerned. By being relaxed, you are showing qualities of unflappable leadership. Ultimately, dogs enjoy each other's company. Given time and space a friendship can emerge from the least likely pairing.

Once a rapport has been established, you can let the dogs move closer together. Eventually they should come up close enough so that they can play together. This is the most natural thing in the world and you should let it happen. The longer this goes on, the better. In time, however, you will need to take the dogs home. When this happens they should all travel together in the car, or whatever kind of transport you are using.

If the existing dog is reluctant to get in the car, owners should put the new dog in first. If tension flares up during the journey, the new dog should be moved to another seat (see page 165 for advice on places to put dogs in the car).

Once you reach home, the dogs must remain on equal status, each of them on a lead. They should be released into the garden at the same time and allowed to get to know each other, but always under supervision.

There is every chance, of course, that the two dogs will not get on immediately. Owners will have to exercise common sense and flexibility. If they get on immediately then they can be allowed to sleep in close proximity to each other from the first night. If they are at each other's throats, however, they must be separated.

The same principle applies over the next few days and weeks. If they are getting along happily, leave them together. If there is friction, separate them. Always err on the side of caution. And always be patient.

In most instances, an eight-week-old dog can settle into a new environment within 48 hours, but there is always a potential for confrontation, so owners should err on the side of caution. Give both the newcomer and the existing dog or dogs their own distinct space during the early days. Be careful too during mealtimes, when clashes could happen.

A SPACE OF ITS OWN

It is important that the dog has its own space, a refuge to which it can retreat when necessary. It doesn't need to be a huge area – as a rule of thumb the dog should be able to lie down on its side with about two inches to spare on either side. There should be a similar amount of space available when it stretches out to full length. What is important is that it is warm, well-insulated and relatively quiet.

There are a variety of options:

- Cages suit many puppies. A lot of puppies seem to respond well to the enclosed, temporary space that they provide. Cages also have the advantage of being transportable and can fit into the back of a car easily. If it ever becomes necessary to discipline the dog for its bad behaviour, the cage can also serve as the equivalent of a child's bedroom, to which it can be banished for a while. However, it's important that the cage doesn't become the puppy's main accommodation. It isn't – and should never be regarded as such. Our dogs should never be forced into cages simply for our own convenience. If it suits the dog to be placed in a cage, that's one thing. It's quite another to put a puppy into a cage for no good reason.
- A kennel with a run is a great option for owners with the available space. This has the added advantage of giving the dog a natural outdoor area where it can exercise itself independently.

🐾 There is a wide range of baskets available, ranging from the simple wicker variety to expensive hand-woven 'designer' baskets. The key is not whether the basket looks good to humans, however. It is far more important that the sleeping area it provides is spacious and comfortable enough for your dog.

🐾 A dog doesn't need an expensive basket, cage or kennel. A home-made den made out of a cardboard box, turned on its side and lined with something soft and soothing, will do the trick provided it creates a safe, secure space for the dog.

A useful tip for making your dog's space comfortable is to put an item of old clothing worn by a member of the family inside the sleeping area. This will not only keep the dog warm, but will also replicate the aromas of its human companions, to add to its sense of safety and security.

A PLACE TO TOILET

A dog that is happy and confident in its toiletting is a dog that is well on the way to leading a well-adjusted life. A dog that isn't is heading for trouble.

By the age of eight weeks, if it comes from a good breeder, the dog should be toilet trained. If it is, then you should allocate a specific toiletting spot, preferably outdoors in a place where whatever is deposited can be absorbed naturally into the earth. There are three key things to remember when choosing this spot.

🐾 Make it as accessible to the dog as possible. If it is outdoors and the dog needs to be let out, be alert to its toilet habits. Always open the door to let the dog out first thing in the morning, for instance, and learn to recognise signs that it needs to go, such as circling near the door.

🐾 Choose somewhere as far away as possible from the dog's sleeping area. A dog is no different to a human in this respect. Who wants to sleep next to their toilet bowl?

🐾 If it is indoors, make sure the toilet area is cleaned regularly.

If a dog is not toilet trained when it arrives in its new home, this should be tackled immediately. You'll have started this process by taking it straight outside to the area you have chosen as soon as you get it home. Stay with the dog while it does its toiletting then praise it with the word you want to use, such as 'empty' or 'clean dog'.

As with everything else during this phase, the key thing is to be patient, and never make a drama out of a crisis. If the dog has an accident, simply scoop up after it and say nothing. If, on the other hand, it succeeds in doing its toiletting in the correct place, be fulsome in your praise and reward it with a tidbit.

Teach the dog to go first thing in the morning. Don't make a big fuss about it. Open the door to the garden or wherever the toilet area has been set up and let the puppy do its business. Then reward it when it has done the necessary.

This should be repeated after each meal – and again when the puppy wakes after a nap. Again the dog should be encouraged to go outside and rewarded when it does what it should do.

As I mentioned earlier, the stress of moving home may cause stomach upsets and diarrhoea. Puppies can dehydrate and deteriorate very quickly, so if this persists for more than 24 hours or becomes severe, you should consult your vet immediately.

NO-GO ZONES

Inevitably, there will be areas of your home where the dog will not be welcome. Bathrooms and toilets, studies and dining rooms, typically, are places humans regard as off limits to their dogs. The key thing is to decide where these areas are early on. Every member of the family should be made aware of the no-go zones so that everyone can enforce the rules.

The best way to ensure a dog doesn't stray into no-go areas, obviously, is to keep the doors closed. If it does find its way into one of these rooms, remove it quietly and quickly with as little fuss as possible. It is entirely likely that the dog will want to follow you everywhere, particularly during the first 48 hours or so. For this reason, children's gates are useful devices within the home. They can divide areas such as the kitchen and the hallway. This works well both for dog and owner. It allows the owner to keep an eye on the dog at all times, and it gives the dog the comfort of being able to see its new guardian too.

The only word of warning is to watch out for the gaps in the gates. If the bars are wide enough apart for a dog to get its head stuck you can be certain it will do precisely that.

There are those who advocate that a dog should not be allowed to climb on to your furniture. There is, however, nothing wrong with this. The only point to remember is that the dog must be invited to join you on a chair or sofa. It shouldn't make the decision independently. If it does jump up without your invitation it should be removed quietly, without any fuss. You can then invite it up. This is an important step towards establishing the first principles of leadership, which we will talk about more in chapter 6.

MAKING THE GARDEN SAFE AND SECURE

If you have a garden, this is clearly going to be an important area for the dog. It is here that it will toilet, do much of its playing and – in time – learn some of the controls it will need before venturing out into the world on walks. As with the home, however, it is important to check the area is secure. Make sure there are no gaps in gates or walls that a young dog could squeeze through. You can be certain its curiosity will get the better of it. As with children's gates, try to ensure there are no spaces in the garden gates or fences – or indeed anywhere else – where a dog could get its head stuck. Given that it will be putting that head into every conceivable nook and crannie of the home during its acclimatisation, you can be fairly certain the worst will happen, so it is best to anticipate it.

THE SMELL OF ITS NEW HOME

A well-adjusted dog from a good breeder should adapt to its new environment relatively easily. It should already be familiar with the smells, sounds and sights of the human environment. If it hasn't been raised well, however – if, say, it has been confined to a shed on a puppy farm for the first eight weeks of its life – then it is going to find the experience overwhelming and may react with fear or anxiety as it comes into contact with new stimuli.

A dog's sense of smell is 100 times stronger than ours and the area of the brain devoted to smell is 14 times as big. It means that in the wild a pack can smell its prey from half a mile away. It is little wonder that we humans have harnessed this incredible ability to help us detect drugs and explosives. Several recent studies have also shown that dogs can sniff out certain cancers in human beings, helping them to get an early diagnosis.

Smell is the first sense dogs acquire so it is no surprise that an eight-week-old puppy is going to be interested in investigating and exploring every smell it encounters in its new world. It will stick its nose everywhere in its new home, so owners acquiring dogs at this age should be ready for this and should ensure the new environment doesn't have any overwhelming smells. A house that smells powerfully – whether it is of cooking, cleaning fluids, smoke or even flowers – can throw a dog into a real panic. Before bringing your puppy home, make sure the home smells as neutral as possible. While handling the dog, too, it is a good idea to avoid using lots of perfume or aftershave.

THE SOUNDS IN ITS NEW HOME

After smell, the dog's most important sense is hearing. They have a far more acute sense of hearing than we humans do. A dog can hear the howl of an adult up to five miles away. They can hear insects inches underground. So it is little wonder they are so agitated by sound.

Arriving in a new home is a massive culture shock for an eight-week-old dog. The house, if you think about it, is full of strange, inexplicable objects capable of making a range of strange, inexplicable noises. You must do all you can to help the puppy acclimatise to those noises. You are not going to achieve this by explaining what each object is because the dog will not understand. What it will understand, however, is that if *you* do not fear that object then, provided it trusts you as its new guardian and protector, it has no reason to be afraid of it either.

If a dog has displayed nervousness on first encountering a particular noise or object – for example, a vacuum cleaner – then that fear should be tackled head on.

For this to work, a baby gate can be a hugely useful asset. It will enable you to keep the dog in a particular area, but at the same time it will allow you to make sure the dog never loses sight of you. Follow these steps to help the dog get used to a vacuum cleaner, or adapt the steps according to the noise it is afraid of, whether it is a doorbell, alarm clock or telephone.

❧ When you are about to vacuum the house, place the dog in the kitchen area behind the baby gate, preferably with another human that it knows and trusts in the same room.

- ❧ Begin vacuuming in the farthest room from the kitchen. If the dog reacts to the sound of the vacuum, the person in the kitchen should encourage the dog to come to it and then hold it. He or she should not be making a huge show of affection. There should be no stroking or talking to the dog. It should just be held in a reassuring way, very calmly so as to show there is nothing to fear.
- ❧ When the first room has been vacuumed, switch the vacuum cleaner off.
- ❧ Repeat the process by switching it back on again in the next room. If the dog reacts, be reassuring once more.
- ❧ Carry on in this way until the vacuum is in the same room as the dog.

This is not a process that is necessarily going to work immediately so you should not rush it. Repetition will get the message across. Usually within a week to ten days, the dog's fear should have lifted.

PUPPY TOYS

Nothing will help settle the dog's nerves better than play, so it is important that a young dog has access to a good supply of toys during these early days. Some of them should be permanently available to it; others will remain in the toybox where you, as leader, will exercise control over their appearance and removal.

This need not entail any great expense for the owner. An eight-week-old dog, with its immature, malleable teeth, will enjoy gnawing away at anything. An old teatowel or blanket soaked in water with a knot tied in it is one of the most popular playthings in my experience.

See pages 88–90 for more advice on playing with your puppy – in particular, ways of using play to reinforce discipline.

＊ ＊ ＊ ＊ ＊ ＊ ＊

There's advice in chapter 8 on dealing with some common behavioural problems. First, though, we are going to look at the basics of feeding, training and grooming your new puppy.

5 | A HEALTHY DIET: THE ESSENTIALS

A healthy, well-balanced diet will be important throughout the dog's life, but it is especially vital for a puppy, who needs the correct nutrients to develop healthy bones, muscles and organs. Many owners will hand over responsibility for their dog's dietary needs to the dog food companies, whose huge range of carefully planned products are scientifically researched so as to provide the right balance of ingredients for dogs. There is nothing wrong with this, but it is still worth understanding the key basic elements that make up a dog's ideal diet and knowing precisely what role they play in our dog's development.

The old saying 'you are what you eat' makes perfect sense. The health and condition of our body is dependent on what we put into it. If we maintain a natural, well-balanced diet containing the nutrients our body needs, we are far less likely to get ill. It is no different for a dog. If we want to maintain a dog's health we need to feed it according to its natural make-up, and the elements that make it what it is. So to understand the basic requirements of a dog's diet we need to know, in simple terms, what a dog consists of and which ingredients it requires to lead a natural, healthy life.

WATER

Just like every other species on earth, the dog relies on water for its existence. It is made up of 70 per cent moisture and it needs a constant supply of water for its organs and systems to function properly. Water performs a variety of roles, from transporting vitamins around the body to cooling the body when it is hot. A dog should never be without a ready supply of clean, fresh water, placed where it can access it at any time.

PROTEINS

Protein is the main component of most of the dog's living tissue, apart from its bones. Its hair, skin, nails and muscles are predominantly protein. Proteins are made up of a variety of amino acids, chemicals that are the essential 'building blocks' of the body. Some amino acids are manufactured naturally in the body, but others have to be provided by the dog's diet. So it is vital that a dog gets a plentiful supply of proteins so as to first grow and then maintain its body in a good state of health with a good muscle tone. By far the most natural source of protein – in every sense – is meat, although large amounts of protein can also be gained from vegetables, eggs, fish, grains and dairy products.

FATS

Fats have two key roles in the body: they provide energy and they also contain essential fatty acids that are needed for many aspects of your dog's health. The two main groups of essential fatty acids are Omega 3 and Omega 6, both of which are associated with helping to maintain a healthy coat and skin. They are also involved in preventing a whole range of medical problems, from allergies and arthritis to heart disease and cancer. Good sources of these essential fatty acids are found in oils, such as evening primrose, fish and linseed.

VITAMINS

Vitamins play an essential role in the growth and development of a healthy dog. They act as catalysts for several crucial chemical reactions, and all have specific roles to play. For example, if your dog manages to cut its paw, one vitamin will help to staunch the bleeding, while another one will go to work repairing the skin. Vitamins come in two forms: those that are soluble in water and those that are soluble in fat. The following are the main vitamins your dog will need.

VITAMIN A

This helps to maintain healthy eyesight and skin. Good sources are liver, milk and egg yolks as well as fish oils.

B VITAMINS

This group of water-soluble vitamins includes B1 (thiamine), B2 (riboflavin), B3 (niacin) and others. They each work to regulate the cell-making processes within the body. Normally they are produced naturally, but occasionally – after a course of antibiotics, for instance – your dog may need to have its levels topped up.

Vitamin B12 helps the development of red blood cells in bone marrow. A good source is meat, such as liver and kidneys, eggs and dairy products. Some breeds, such as Giant Schnauzers, can be born with a condition that prevents them absorbing B12 properly and may need special injections of the vitamin throughout their life.

VITAMIN C

This is an antioxidant that acts against 'free radicals' and also helps the generation of Vitamin E. Dogs should not be given too much Vitamin C, however. It can seep into the dog's urine and form into bladder sand or stones.

VITAMIN D

By maintaining the balance of calcium and phosphate in the body, this vitamin helps the formation of healthy bones and teeth. A deficiency of Vitamin D can cause rickets. This is rare, however, because Vitamin D is present in virtually all prepared dog foods.

VITAMIN E

This maintains the dog's immune system by reducing the levels of cell-destroying 'free radicals' that can lead to diseases like cancer. It also helps prevent skin diseases, heart and neurological problems.

MINERALS

Around four per cent of a dog is made up of minerals, basic chemical elements that either form solid structures like the bones and teeth, or bodily fluids, in particular the blood. It is essential that dogs have the right levels of each of these minerals if they are to develop into healthy adults, and in particular have good, strong teeth and bones.

CALCIUM AND PHOSPHORUS

These two minerals aid the development of strong teeth and bones and help the nervous system too. Imbalances in one or the other can be a problem. In general, dogs' diets should include marginally more calcium than phosphorus. The ideal ratio is 1.2–1.4 parts calcium to 1 part phosphorus.

MAGNESIUM

Magnesium helps maintain the right balance of calcium and phosphorus, which in turn helps keep the dog's skeleton healthy. It also aids muscle and nerve functions.

SELENIUM

This mineral maintains some types of body tissue, such as the heart muscles. It can be toxic in even low levels so should only form a very small part of a dog's diet.

COPPER AND IRON

These two elements work to transport oxygen around the body in the form of red blood cells.

ZINC

The correct level of zinc ensures healthy skin and an efficient immune system. At the same time, it helps the taste buds to function properly.

IODINE

A dog must have enough of this mineral in its system to allow the hormone-producing thyroid gland to work properly. Without the right level, hormones can become imbalanced causing problems.

OTHER ESSENTIAL INGREDIENTS IN A HEALTHY DIET

FIBRE

An essential element of a dog's diet, this stimulates the production of saliva and the gastric juices. It is also a valuable protection against a host of medical problems, from constipation and obesity to diabetes and bowel disorders. In the wild, the wolf gets fibre from the fur and intestines of its carrion. The domestic dog's best sources of soluble fibre are cooked vegetables and rice, which have the added benefit of being 'sticky', so that they remain in the stomach longer, allowing more time for their goodness to be absorbed. Dry, insoluble fibre comes in the form of bran, which is commonly found in breakfast cereal. A dog's fibre needs may vary through the years. Older dogs in particular may need more fibre in their diets so as to help their bowels function efficiently.

CARBOHYDRATES

Carbohydrates are compounds made up of sugars called monosaccharides. The dog's body is able to convert these to provide almost immediate energy and to store reserve energy in the form of glycogen. Good sources of carbohydrate include grain, rice, corn and wheat.

BONES

In the wild, the wolf maintains its teeth and gums by ripping and gnawing at the carcasses of its prey. The bones also provide it with all the calcium it needs. Since it assimilated itself into the human world, however, feeding in this way hasn't been an option for the dog.

Modern dog foods provide dogs with all the calcium they need. But as a dog gets older and develops its adult teeth, it is going to need something that provides those teeth and gums with a good workout. Bones provide the perfect option, especially as they are also tasty, exercise the jaws and can keep dogs happily occupied for hours on end.

Make sure you don't give bones before the second teeth have come through at the age of four or five months. Until then, get your puppy to chew on a damp towel or rope toy. And once the adult teeth have come through, owners should ensure their dogs only chew on the healthier, raw, marrow bones. Preferably you should ask your butcher for raw, beef marrow bones. You should also make sure you give your dog strong, hard bones that will not splinter. Avoid bones taken from a cooked piece of meat like lamb or pork or from chicken. These are too soft and can easily splinter, blocking or tearing the dog's digestive system once digested, or getting stuck in the throat and choking your dog. Alternatively you can give your dog a chew made from animal hide which you can get from any good pet shop. Again be aware that they can fragment after repeated chewing and should be discarded regularly.

FEEDING YOUR DOG – THE OPTIONS

Dogs need a balanced diet that contains the mix of protein, fat, vitamins and minerals their bodies demand. Precisely how these dietary needs are met, however, is a matter for the owner, and there are several options.

HOME-MADE FOOD

Many owners like the idea of cooking for their dog. This is laudable, of course, but they should be aware that it is a complex job. For a balanced diet a dog doesn't just need the right mix of ingredients; it also needs them in the correct proportions to each other.

It is easy, for instance, to imagine that a dog – as the descendant of the wolf – will happily survive on a diet of pure protein in the form of meat. This overlooks, of course, the fact that in the wild wolves eat not just the muscle but the bones, internal organs, intestinal contents, skin and hair of their carrion as well. It is in these that they find many of the essential nutrients they need. If a dog were fed a purely meat diet, it would be deficient in a range of elements, including vitamins A and D and calcium.

Having said all this, it is perfectly possible to come up with a well-researched diet. Recipes based on a simple mix of chicken, liver, rice, bone meal, salt and sunflower or corn oil can work quite well. A pinch of garlic can also be good for the dog's circulatory system. In the age of the internet there is a lot of information and recipes available.

Any owner contemplating making home-made food, however, must be prepared for a lot of hard work, especially as its dog's needs are going to be changing through their life.

PREPARED FOODS

It is no surprise that the vast majority of dog owners place their dog's dietary welfare in the hands of the major food manufacturers. They have put huge resources into researching and understanding the complex mechanism that is the dog's body. As a result they have produced a range of foods that satisfy all the owner's main concerns. On the whole their foods provide the right balance of protein, fat, vitamins and minerals a dog needs to remain fit and healthy. These foods come in a huge range of recipes, a variety of textures and forms, all of them highly convenient. They also reflect the different needs of dogs at different times in their lives, with puppies, in particular, very well catered for.

Prepared dog foods come with guarantees of quality, nutrition and safety. Since the introduction of mandatory nutritional labelling, owners can monitor precisely what their dogs are eating by looking at the packets.

Prepared foods come in two different categories – complete and complementary. These should never be mixed.

Each has its own merits.

- Complete food, as the name suggests, provides an all-in-one balanced diet made up of all the essential nutrients in the right proportions. The dog will not need to eat anything else to maintain good health. Complete foods are available for every key stage of the dog's life, from puppyhood and the early growth stages, through to specially designed foods for pregnant mothers and elderly dogs.
- Complementary food is designed to be eaten alongside other foods, such as biscuit mixers or canned meat. The two are combined to give the dog the balanced diet it needs.

Within both of these categories there are two types of prepared food: dry and wet.

- Increasingly popular, dry foods have the advantage of being relatively inexpensive and very convenient. They have basically been cooked under pressure then dried out. Fat and preservatives are added to make them tastier for the dog. They can be served dry or softened up with the addition of water. They are also more economical and last longer.
- By contrast, wet foods have retained some of the moisture from the ingredients. These foods are served in a soft form, usually in a tin. They can be complete or complementary.

Which of the options an owner goes for is a matter of personal choice, but a few factors should be borne in mind.

- 🐾 Soft or wet food is more easily digestible, but it will place a greater onus on the owner to care for the dog's teeth (see pages 142–7). Wet food doesn't give the teeth a workout and allows tartar to build. Gum diseases like gingivitis can easily take hold.
- 🐾 Many of the modern dry foods have been designed specifically to give the teeth a workout. The good ones release minerals that become embedded in the plaque of the teeth and block the build-up of tartar.
- 🐾 Some smaller dogs may have problems crunching on some of the hard 'kibbles' that make up dried foods. You can overcome this by soaking them in water.

The key thing from an owner's point of view is that you read the instructions on the packaging of these meals carefully. They usually contain detailed plans for feeding dogs of different ages and sizes, with precise measures and feeding times. In the main, you should stick to what they say.

NATURE'S NUTRITION: THE BARF DIET

There is a growing body of people who feed their dogs a very different diet, the so-called Bones and Raw Food, or BARF, diet. They believe this is by far the most healthy – and natural – way of eating for the dog. Not everyone agrees with them, but for me, at least, their argument is a persuasive one.

MAKE-UP OF A TYPICAL DOG FOOD
AMOUNT CONTAINED WITHIN FOOD AS PERCENTAGE

NUTRIENT	FUNCTION	AVERAGE/ SMALL DOG	LARGE DOG
Protein	Vital element to build healthy tissues, organs and muscles	28	30
Fat	Supplies energy, essential fatty acids for nerve function and healthy cells	18	11
Carbohydrate	Supplies energy	37	43
Fibre	Encourages and maintains healthy digestive system	2.5	2.7
Moisture	Essential nutrient, 70 per cent of body	7.5	7.5
Calcium	Aids strong teeth and bones, helps nerve function	1.3	1
Phosphorus	Helps strong bones and energy production	1	0.8
Sodium	Aids fluid balance and nerve function	0.5	0.5
Potassium	Fluid balance, nerve function and muscle contraction	0.75	0.75
Magnesium	Healthy bones, nerve and enzyme function	0.1	0.1

NUTRIENT	FUNCTION	AVERAGE/ SMALL DOG	LARGE DOG
Omega-3 fatty acids	Aids healthy skin and glossy coat	0.4	0.25
Omega-6 fatty acids	Aids healthy skin and glossy coat	3.4	2.5

This table illustrates how a typical complete dog food reflects the essential ingredients that constitute a dog's make-up. Our dogs literally eat what they are. Source: Hill's Pet Nutrition

Dog food, at least as we know it today, is a recent invention. It has been around for 100 years or less. So how on earth did dogs not only survive but thrive before this? The answer to that is, of course, by eating what came naturally. For tens of thousands of years dogs lived off food they had hunted or scavenged for themselves. In their very early days they hunted in packs. Their natural prey would be herbivores, such as rabbits, deer or sheep. At other times they would scavenge the leftovers from bigger animals brought down by bigger hunters, such as lions or bears. They would supplement this diet by grazing during the summertime. They were then – as now – opportunistic eaters. They took what they could get, when they could get it.

Yet this diet provided dogs with a whole range of proteins and nutrients. By eating everything from the soft tissue and offal to the skin, they helped maintain their condition and warded off sickness too. By eating the carcasses of other animals down to the bones and hair, they gave their teeth the rigorous workout they needed and supplemented them with calcium.

When man first domesticated the dog it was easy for them to maintain this diet. In exchange for their hunting skills, dogs were left to eat everything their human companions didn't want – which, as it happened, was quite a lot. Dogs maintained their natural diet throughout their early days with man. It was another reason why the partnership worked so well for them.

It was only when man created an industrialised society that things went awry. Suddenly man and dog were no longer sharing meals together. Man ate everything he wanted, and there were no longer any leftovers. Instead he invented foods that he believed would be of benefit to the dog.

There are many who think that by returning to their natural foods dogs receive a much more rounded and healthy diet. For a start, they argue that the mere act of cooking or processing food removes up to 70 per cent of its nutritional value. But they also argue that many common diseases – from tooth decay and bad breath to colitis and kidney disease, skin problems and rheumatoid arthritis – are a result of deficiency in the modern, manmade foods. People who feed their dog the BARF diet say their dogs are leaner, fitter, better conditioned and muscled animals. For these reasons they recommend at least partially returning dogs to their natural way of eating.

SO WHAT IS A NATURAL DIET?

The essential ingredients of a raw diet are raw meat, liquidised raw fruit and vegetables, and raw bones. Dogs should be fed those according to the following principles.

- 🐾 They should eat 100–150g of meat a day for every 10kg of their weight.
- 🐾 They should be given a variety of meats to benefit from the different nutrients. Pork is the only meat to be avoided, although beef should be avoided if the dog has a skin or bowel problem.
- 🐾 Offal, such as kidney, heart, lung or liver, should replace meat once a week.
- 🐾 They should eat 200–300g of fruit and vegetables a day for every 10kg of their weight.
- 🐾 The fruit and vegetable part of the meal can be supplemented by nuts, herbs and cooked beans.
- 🐾 Feed dogs raw bones at least once a week to exercise teeth.
- 🐾 Do not feed dogs cereals.

HOW AND WHEN TO INTRODUCE
A DOG TO A NATURAL DIET

In the wild, puppies are introduced to raw food almost immediately. At first their mother or other pack members will give it to them in the form of regurgitated or chewed food, but they will soon be eating on their own. There is no reason why a domestic dog can't be weaned onto a natural diet just as quickly. The only thing to be careful of is bones. As well as the danger of brittle bones that can splinter and choke a dog, owners should be wary when feeding them poultry, such as chicken. Make sure there aren't any small, sharp bones as these can easily get stuck in the throat and cause choking. Fish can also be a very occasional part of a puppy's diet, but should always be cooked carefully and filleted of all bones.

If you acquire a dog that has not been fed on a natural diet, you should take care to make any transition to BARF gradual. Introduce one or two natural meals a week to begin with. Then, once the dog's system has begun to get used to this, increase the number of natural meals slowly until they account for the dog's whole diet.

BUILDING UP A PUPPY'S DIET

As it grows, a puppy's appetite will increase accordingly. In the first week or so of weaning the puppy should have three feeds a day. By the second week, when it is four weeks old, this should increase to five feeds a day.

The key is to feed the puppy a little but often. This way it is not going to have any digestive problems. This should be wound down gradually, with the dog eating less frequently but in greater volume. By 12 weeks it should be down to four meals a day. By 14 weeks it should be three a day. By the time it's five months it should be down to two meals a day, a morning breakfast and an evening meal.

FEEDING BY EYE

Of course all dogs are different so, no matter how precise the manufacturer's instructions on food labels, every owner will have to make judgements on the precise quantities of food their dogs get. This requires owners to be vigilant and to feed by eye – using your own observations about your dog's needs – as well as by the packet or the tin.

One of the biggest problems with puppies – and indeed all dogs – is overfeeding. It is easy to see if a dog is carrying too much or too little weight. The shoulders are often the most obvious sign. Puppies can put on weight here so that they seem to have no neck. This is to be avoided, because it can cause diarrhoea and other problems. If a puppy does develop diarrhoea, withhold food for 24 hours. Don't worry; it won't starve.

By the same token, under-feeding can result in rapid weight loss. Look out for protruding ribs or thin backs. If this happens, simply increase the number of meals per day rather than the volume of food served at each. As with all stages of a dog's development, any changes must be introduced gradually.

In chapter 13, there are instructions on body scoring your dog, a system of monitoring its height and weight (see pages 185–7).

6 | THE FOUNDATION STONES OF TRAINING

Having a puppy is fun – there is no getting away from that – but it is also a responsibility, one that you will have to meet for many years to come. It is vital that you waste no time in giving yourself the tools you are going to need to live up to that responsibility, and by that I mean controls.

As your relationship with your puppy progresses, you will need to be able to exercise more and more control over its behaviour. When you eventually take your puppy out into the wider world on its first walks, at around 14 weeks of age, it is going to be up to you to protect and guide it. You need to be able to get it to sit, to come, and to walk to heel. Unless you are able to exercise some basic controls, your dog will be at considerable risk. This is a fundamental part of your responsibility as an owner, so it is crucial that you begin to introduce the foundation stones of training early on in the puppy's life. The hard work starts here!

CANINE COMMUNICATION: THE FIRST STEPS

As we have seen already, a dog operates according to the same rules as its ancient ancestor, the wolf. All dogs are hard-wired to believe in the power of the pack, and the importance of having a hierarchy that preserves that pack. As a puppy moves away from its mother and the litter and begins to interact with the extended pack that is its human family, it needs to find a leader with whom it is comfortable, one in whom it can place its trust.

In the wild, this information would be provided by means of clear and unambiguous signals from both the alpha pair and the members considered subordinate within the pack's pecking order. They would leave the young pup in no doubt as to its place in the pecking order. And the alpha pair would make it clear it is them in whom it should place its trust.

Of course, the domestic dog lives in a world designed by and run by humans, so it is not surprising they can be extremely confused by the pack they find themselves inhabiting. To make matters worse, without realising it some owners give out signals that lead their dogs to the wrong conclusions about the hierarchy of their pack. As a result, dogs can develop mistaken ideas about their status within the domestic pack and set themselves up for a whole host of behavioural problems further down the road.

Your job as an owner is to ensure that the dog knows clearly that you are at the top of the hierarchy: that you are always the leader of your domestic pack. By establishing this now, when your dog is still in its puppyhood, and remaining consistent you will help to ensure that it regards you as its leader for the rest of its life.

Your puppy should have been introduced to the idea that humans are at the head of the social hierarchy before it arrives in your home. Good breeders will slowly and almost subliminally have introduced the idea that they are the leaders. The first steps are taken at three weeks during the first interaction, then during weaning and the first grooming sessions. By taking charge of playtime, too, they underline their status.

Each time you interact with your dog, you are conveying an important message: I am responsible for your welfare, and you can trust me to fulfil that responsibility. The young dog will already have elevated the breeder to a position above it in the pack. It is now up to you to continue this association. You too must establish yourself as the leader, and to do this you must introduce the first of the basic controls you will need in order to keep the dog safe in the wider world.

The good news is that there is a simple set of signals that an owner can use to communicate the key messages a dog needs to receive. By learning these signals, owners can not only avoid confusing their dogs, but more importantly they can establish themselves as leaders from an early age. And the benefits of this are enormous.

There are four key signals, each of them based on ones used in the wild. To understand them, we need to understand first how they work in the natural world.

THE FOUR RITUALS

A pack is always subtly testing its leaders, asking it small questions that require them to show they are still in charge. On a day-to-day basis, the most frequent opportunity the alpha pair get to do this is when the pack reunites after a separation. The pair have their own personal space, a comfort zone within which they operate. They effectively say 'don't call us, we'll call you'. No other wolf is allowed to encroach into this space unless invited to do so. When the pack assembles, the alpha pair remain in this space until they are ready to receive their junior members. When they are ready – and only when they are ready – subordinates can approach to pay homage.

It is not a point that needs to be made for any great length of time. When they are satisfied the pack has accepted their leadership once more, the alphas will allow the subordinates to approach them. But they will not do so until they are satisfied they are being paid the respect they are due. It is a simple yet hugely powerful way for the alpha pair to re-establish their primacy in the pack, without ever resorting to cruelty, confrontation or violence.

Unsurprisingly, food provides two of the other key methods for underlining the alphas' status. The first great opportunity to assert themselves in this way comes during the hunt. This operation requires a combination of organisation, determination, tactics and management skill. It is the alpha's job to provide all these qualities. It is they who search for the hunting grounds and they who direct the chase and direct the 'kill'. It is the job of the subordinates to play their part and provide support. Again, any questioning of their authority will not be tolerated.

Once the 'kill' has been executed, the alphas generally underline their status by getting first refusal on the carrion. Only when they are satisfied and signal their feed is over will the rest of the pack be permitted to eat – and then according to the strict pecking order of the pack, with the senior subordinates feasting first and the juniors last. Back at the camp, the pups and baby-sitters will be fed by the hunters' regurgitation of their food. Again, this makes perfect sense to the pack. After all, its survival depends on the alphas remaining in peak physical condition.

The final area in which the alpha pair show their leadership comes during times of perceived danger. Whenever danger threatens, it is their role to protect the pack at all costs. The pair do this unblinkingly and with the authority their pack expects of them, reacting in one of three ways: running away, ignoring the threat or defending themselves. (The three Fs: Flight, Freeze or Fight.) Whichever response the alpha pair selects, the pack will back up their leader to the hilt.

THE FOUR QUESTIONS AN OWNER MUST ASK

If we accept that a domestic dog believes it is part of a pack, then we must also accept that it is looking at all times for someone to step up to the plate and lead that pack. In a world designed and occupied by humans, that leader has to be a human. It is not a responsibility a dog can meet, no matter how intelligent it may be. If a dog is led to believe it is in charge, it will lead to all manner of problems.

The key to owning a happy and well-adjusted dog is understanding that you – not it – must be the leader. And the key to establishing this early on lies in taking charge of the four key areas through which dogs communicate.

The key to establishing yourself as owner lies in dealing with the domestic dog's equivalent of the wolf pack's four rituals. Specifically, the owner must answer the following four questions.

🐾 When the pack reunites after a separation, who is in charge?

🐾 When the pack faces a perceived danger, who will protect the puppy?

🐾 When the pack goes on the hunt, who will lead them?

🐾 When the pack eats, who will eat first?

An owner must ensure that the dog sees him or her – and ultimately every other member of the household – as the answer to each of those questions. And they must make sure that the dog reaches these conclusions of its own free will, without any coercion or violence.

BASIC CONTROLS – THE COME

The life of an eight-week-old dog is remarkably simple. Sleeping, eating and playing dominate its thinking. Owners can capitalise on the last two of these over-riding instincts to introduce the first of the key commands the dog needs to learn – the come. This should be introduced soon after the first 48 hours, when the dog has settled into its new environment.

1. Plan to do this for the first time after the dog has eaten. Be prepared with a supply of tidbits, such as small pieces of dried meat or cheese, which you will use as food rewards.
2. When the dog has finished its meal and begins playing, call it by name.
3. When it gives you the telltale 'are you talking to me?' look, squat or kneel, extend your hand with the food reward visible and ask the dog to 'come', in a warm, inviting voice.
4. If the dog doesn't move towards you initially, stretch your hand further to make the food reward more visible – and to make the smell more recognisable.
5. When the dog comes over, reward it and give it quiet praise. Don't be too effusive; just let it know it has done a good job
6. Stroke or ruffle the dog's neck area, to underline leadership (touching this vulnerable area is a powerful signal of leadership in the wild).

If the dog rushes or jumps up, or alternatively rolls over expecting to be tickled, get up and walk away immediately. Do the same if the dog does not respond to the invitation after a couple of minutes: go away and get on with your day, then try again a few hours later after the next feed. Remain patient. It will respond eventually and when it does you will have laid an important foundation stone.

BASIC CONTROLS – THE SIT

The ability to get your dog to sit is going to be a useful tool. You will need it during grooming and whenever you or your vet is administering medicine, so it is important you introduce this basic control early on.

You want your dog to repeat this procedure easily for the rest of its life. But you don't want it to do so because it is frightened or feels somehow threatened. You want it to happen voluntarily, because the dog knows it is a good thing. Dogs are – like humans – essentially selfish creatures. They work on a 'what's in it for me?' basis. So the only way your dog is going to sit of its own free will is if it makes a positive association with sitting from an early stage. Once more, using food rewards is the key to achieving this initially.

1. Take a tidbit, show it to the dog then bring it towards and then over its head. As you are doing this, say the word 'sit' in a kind, warm, unthreatening voice.
2. The dog should follow the food with its eyes and as it does so, its natural reflex will be to arch its neck backwards so that its whole body tips back and it ends up sitting down.
3. The moment its bottom touches the ground, reward the dog with fulsome praise, stroking it and giving it the food reward.
4. Dogs are not mind readers, so if it does not respond the first time try again, and again if necessary, remaining calm and patient.

Wolf pups at four-and-a-half weeks old.

CT scans of (left to right) a Grey Wolf, a Great Dane and a Dachshund reveal a skeleton that has remained unchanged in its basic construction.

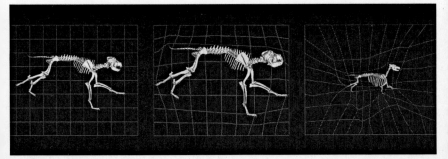

With playtime over, the litter sleeps in an exhausted heap.

Young dogs should quickly adapt from mother's milk to solid meals soon after they reach three weeks of age.

A puppy needs to feel safe, comfortable and happy in its new environment.

Chewing strips provide the young dog's emerging teeth with the exercise they need to grow and remain healthy.

The way a puppy reacts to being handled will give a strong indication of its personality, and a puppy that happily allows itself to be cradled is more likely to be a contented and relaxed dog.

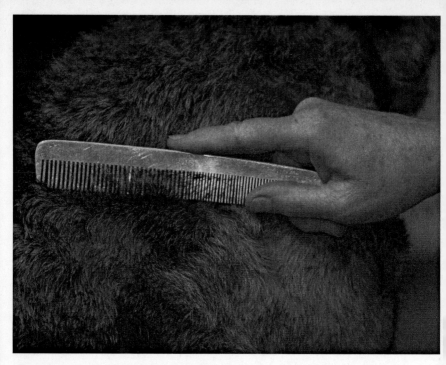

Short-haired dogs should have their coats combed through thoroughly on a regular basis.

Every area of a long-haired dog's body needs careful grooming, including their ears.

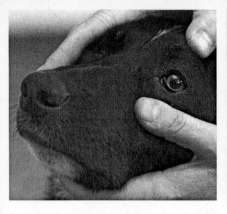

Regular inspection of the eyes should reveal early signs of diseases.

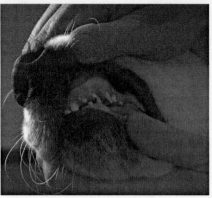

Teeth should also be checked regularly.

Dew claws need careful checking to avoid potential infection.

Regular claw clipping should begin at around three weeks old.

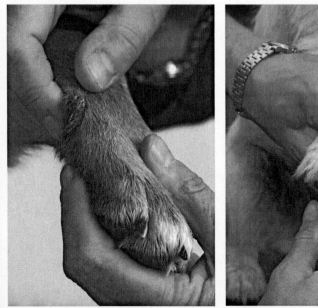

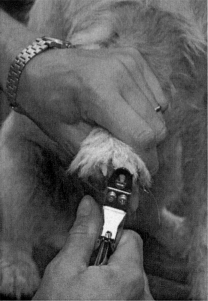

Exploring the world.

Right: Gently does it.

Middle right: A new sensation.

Far right: Taking it slowly.

'Sit!'

'Good dog!'

The Boston Terrier's cropped ears seems to signal that it is constantly alert.

With their broad shoulders and chests and their forward-leaning stance, bulldogs can convey a threatening message to other dogs.

A Basset Hound naturally carries its tail high, which can send a confusing signal to other breeds.

Other dogs can be deeply confused by the Old English Sheepdog's seeming absence of eyes, ears, a tail or a foreface.

5. If, when you pass the food over its head, the dog shuffles backwards rather than sitting, place it with its back to something solid, such as a door or a wall, so that it can't move backwards.

   If it still refuses to comply, very gently place a hand behind the dog so that you are just touching its bottom, then pass the food over again, using the hand as a stop, just as you would support a baby before it learns to sit on its own.

6. When you have successfully got the dog to sit, repeat this process once or twice to imprint it in its memory.

The three elements – the word 'sit', the act of tipping over on to its bottom and the food reward – will now be inextricably and positively linked in the dog's mind and you should be able to ask it to sit whenever you need it to.

CONTROLLING THE CONTROLLER

It's worth making the point that you should use the basic controls sparingly at first. You definitely shouldn't ask the dog to sit each time it comes to you. The reasons for this are simple: dogs are highly manipulative creatures and may use the fact they have grasped these principles – and your obvious delight at the fact they have done so – to their advantage. It is quite possible your dog will place itself at your feet, volunteering to sit, on a regular basis, but it is crucial you don't respond to this. Remember: one of the key purposes of controls is to underline your status as leader. By allowing the dog to decide when it sits – and gets a food reward – you are relinquishing that status. You are letting it control you, the controller. So be careful.

USING FOOD POWER TO INSTIL DISCIPLINE

Food is one of the most powerful tools available in terms of signalling. In the wild, every pack member understands that food is earned. It is not a right. This same message must be inculcated early on in a dog's life. The dog must learn the following principles.

- 🐾 Food does not just turn up; it has to be earned.
- 🐾 The person who provides the food is the surrogate protector it is looking for.
- 🐾 There are certain ways to behave when food is being eaten

All these points must be reinforced from the outset.

There are some simple rules when feeding puppies. The four main ones relate to things you definitely should *not* do.

DON'T LET DOGS EAT BETWEEN MEALS

Dogs are opportunistic eaters. If they see a chance to grab a snack, they will take it. This, of course, undermines the principle that you are trying to introduce – that you are the sole provider of food – so it can't be allowed. It's important to explain this to other members of the family and indeed visitors to the house. Simply by slipping your dog a tidbit, a visitor could set your dog's progress back by weeks.

DON'T STICK TO SET MEAL TIMES

Dogs are smart, and if you adhere to strict feeding times they will quickly work out when to expect a meal. Instead, you should deliberately mix up meal times so that they don't anticipate them. This way you will ensure the messages you want to communicate with the dogs – that is, *I* am the leader, *I* choose when we eat – always come through loud and clear.

DON'T LET THE DOG GET TOO EXCITED

Meal times offer an excellent chance to introduce principles of good behaviour, so they must be calm and controlled affairs. Because its sense of smell is so strong, a dog will be drawn to the kitchen or feeding area the minute you start preparing its meal. If it starts leaping around and generally being over-excited, wait. You don't need to speak; just stand quietly with the food on the worktop, away from the dog, until it calms down. Only then should you continue to serve the meal. When you do so you should walk away, underlining the point that – as leader – you have decided it is now the dog's turn to eat.

DON'T ALLOW THE DOG TO WALK
AWAY FROM ITS FOOD

Your dog must learn that it has no control over meal times. So while it is acceptable for it to stand up from its bowl to digest its meal, it is definitely not acceptable for it to walk away before the meal is finished. If it does this you must remove the bowl immediately. When the dog returns it must not be offered the food again. It needs to learn that meal time is precisely that – it is not time to go off for a walk or to be distracted by other things. This may seem harsh, but it is a lesson that will be learned very quickly.

THE POWER OF PLAY

Just as in the wild, play provides the puppy with some of the most powerful information it will receive during this phase of its life. It will learn what it can and cannot get away with physically. It will learn about its status within the household, and how to recognise the status of others. Your puppy will have learnt much during its eight weeks playing within in its litter, and this education process needs to continue in its new home.

Play provides an owner with a crucial opportunity to establish their relationship with their puppies, as it can offer a powerful signal about hierarchy. It can also establish the owner as a fun leader. Yet, if you are not careful, it could set some misleading precedents. This is a relationship that may last for life, so it is vital that play is conducted according to certain rules. Essentially, there are three 'don'ts'.

DON'T LET THE PUPPY DICTATE PLAYTIME
The sight of a puppy appearing with a ball in its mouth is guaranteed to melt most hearts, but owners must not instinctively start playing straight away. Responding to this will

plant the idea that playtime is something the puppy instigates. And this, in time, will help instil the idea that the puppy is the leader. It is not, and it must be made apparent that it is not from this early stage.

DON'T ENCOURAGE TUGGING GAMES

This is setting up a problem for later down the line because it is a challenge to leadership. If the puppy gets away with it once or twice, it could begin to develop false ideas about its status. It's also encouraging the puppy to bite harder, which can make matters even worse. What is a fun game with a puppy is not so funny with a fully grown dog, especially if it's a big breed.

DON'T TOLERATE BITING

Anything that encourages a puppy to bite humans is to be avoided at this point. It will lead to a positive association and may leave the dog thinking it's acceptable behaviour for the rest of its life. This is why dogs whose job it will be to bite – such as police dogs – aren't taught to bite until they are 18 months of age.

The key to this is understanding that biting is not an aggressive act on the puppy's part. It is not trying to bite – it is trying to hold on, just as it did when playing with its siblings in the litter. The key to stopping it is not to make a drama of it. Humans tend to panic when a puppy nips, but this will only make matters worse. The thing to do is to give a little yell as a sibling would do, then immediately walk away. If the puppy chases after you and grabs at your trousers or dress, remove it and put it behind the baby gate or into another room. Leave it there for a reasonable length of time – up to an hour. Do this without ceremony and don't worry about being hard on the dog. It's not hard; in fact, it's very positive. As an owner you have learned there is a cut-off point and the puppy has learned for the first time about the consequences of its actions.

❧ ❧ ❧ ❧ ❧ ❧ ❧

There may be some behavioural problems to contend with in the first few days and weeks of your puppy's life in its new home, especially if it has come from a puppy farm or some other difficult background rather than a reputable breeder, but with gentle perseverance, and adherence to the basic rules you have set, these should be overcome. See chapter 8 for more advice on behavioural problems.

7 | GROOMING: THE KEY TO GOOD HEALTH

The importance of grooming cannot be overstated. It is about much more than making sure a dog looks its best at all times. First and foremost, it is a vital way of maintaining and monitoring a dog's health. The coat is susceptible to all manner of threats and needs to be cared for at all times. Grooming gives you a chance to perform a number of routine checks on the dog's welfare.

In addition it provides a perfect way to form a valuable bond of trust between pet and owner early in life, and allows the owner to underline the dog's status within the domestic hierarchy.

During grooming, the owner will touch the dog's most vulnerable areas, something that in the wild only an alpha would be able to do. Similarly, while grooming, the owner takes over the cleaning and maintenance work that dogs naturally do themselves, again a signal of superiority within the pecking order. It also puts the owner in a position of physical dominance, standing over the dog. For all these reasons, grooming is something that should begin as early as possible in the dog's life.

A good breeder will have got your puppy used to being touched in sensitive areas such as the mouth and the feet, and to roll its head to one side so you can look in its ears. If your puppy has not been conditioned in this way, start following the instructions on pages 15–16 twice a day and it should soon become used to it.

A dog's coat is the first line of defence against many diseases. It is made up of two kinds of hair – protective 'guard' hair and fine, heat-preserving 'down' hair. Centuries of breeding has, of course, produced dogs with very different mixtures of hair. German Shepherds, for example, have a coat dominated by 'guard' hair.

In the wild, wolves look after their own skin and coat by rolling around in dust or sand. This not only massages the coat but also dislodges any accumulated debris and stimulates the skin to produce sebum, an oily substance that naturally protects the skin and hair from infection. Our dogs may occasionally use this method to keep themselves clean, but in general they rely on licking themselves. This isn't enough, particularly given the array of invisible ailments that a dog faces in the human world. So it is up to us to monitor and maintain our dog's coats.

GROOMING DIFFERENT TYPES OF COAT

The principles of grooming are the same regardless of which type of coat your dog has. The object of the exercise is to remove any dead hair and to clean the living hair and the skin, stimulating the oil-producing glands in the skin to lubricate the coat so that it looks sleek and healthy. This should be achieved without hurting or causing the dog any distress.

There are a few guiding principles.

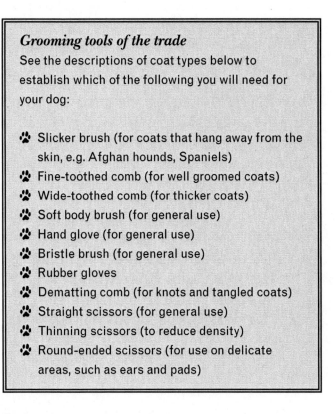

Grooming tools of the trade

See the descriptions of coat types below to establish which of the following you will need for your dog:

- Slicker brush (for coats that hang away from the skin, e.g. Afghan hounds, Spaniels)
- Fine-toothed comb (for well groomed coats)
- Wide-toothed comb (for thicker coats)
- Soft body brush (for general use)
- Hand glove (for general use)
- Bristle brush (for general use)
- Rubber gloves
- Dematting comb (for knots and tangled coats)
- Straight scissors (for general use)
- Thinning scissors (to reduce density)
- Round-ended scissors (for use on delicate areas, such as ears and pads)

- Don't tug at the dog's hair when grooming. If a section of coat is really matted and knotted and can't be teased out with a light brush, cut it away with scissors rather than tugging at it for minutes on end. There is no need to make the dog suffer.
- When selecting a bristle brush, test it on the back of your hand before using it on the dog. If it hurts your skin then it is going to hurt the dog's, so don't use it.

⚙ When grooming male dogs, take care to protect their
genitals. Cup the dog's testes in your spare hand while
grooming the area, or you may hurt it.

Different types of coats require specific treatment, and the
main brushing should be carried out according to the advice
for the type of dog you have, as outlined in the categories
below.

SMOOTH COATS

There are two types of smooth coat: the short, fine coats of
dogs such as Whippets and Boxers and the longer, denser
coats of Labradors and Corgis. In general, this is the easiest
group of dogs to groom. They should be groomed on average
once a week. The longer coats can be groomed with a comb
appropriate to the coat's condition and a bristle brush, while
a hand glove or rubber glove is enough to care for the shorter
coats. Use a dematting comb to remove minor matting and
tangles.

Any bits of debris that remain stuck in the coat can be
removed by softening them with a little cooking oil. Particular
care should also be taken with the undercoat of the longer-
coated dogs.

WIRY COATS

Dogs falling into this category include most of the Terrier
family and the wire-haired Dachshund and Schnauzer. They
should be groomed twice a week without fail, in much the
same way as the coats of Labradors and Corgis, with an

appropriate comb and bristle brush. Matting is a particular problem with this type of coat so great care should be taken to remove every gnarled and knotted section. Avoid tugging; if necessary, cut away the affected area of the coat with scissors.

In addition to this regular grooming, the top coat should be stripped and plucked, preferably by a professional, every 12 weeks or so, and this should be followed by a good bath (see pages 97–100). If you prefer, the dog can be machine-clipped every six to eight weeks. Be aware that machine-clipping only deals with the length and not the density. This means the coat doesn't look after itself as naturally as it should and will cause problems in the long term.

Wiry coats also grow around the eyes and ears, where they should be carefully clipped with scissors.

LONG COATS

These coats are found on Collies, German Shepherds and Old English Sheepdogs, amongst other breeds. Grooming of long-coated dogs should start with a general detangling with a slicker brush followed by a thorough combing through with a comb appropriate to the coat and condition. Finally, the coat should be combed through with a wide-toothed comb. Particular care should be taken to comb thoroughly the dense hair on the legs, chest, tail and hindquarters. These dogs need to be groomed on a daily basis, and trimmed of excess hair once a month at least. Again, bad knotting should be cut out.

CURLY, NON-MOULTING COATS

This type of coat is found on dogs such as the Poodle and the Bichon Frise. Unlike every other type of coat, it doesn't moult, which makes caring for – and managing – it all the more important. They should be brushed through on a daily basis with a specialised 'dematting' comb, with particular attention paid to the outsides of the ears and the feet.

The most important thing is that these coats are clipped every six to eight weeks. This is best left to a professional groomer. The groomer should also look out for the hair that tends to grow inside the dog's ear canal and can cause problems if not maintained properly.

SILKY COATS

Afghan Hounds, Lhasa Apsos, Spaniels and Yorkshire Terriers are among the diverse group of dogs that have a silky coat. They require a lot of care and attention because these coats can quickly become a tangled mess and need regular brushing and bathing to avoid becoming matted. Some breeds, such as the Maltese and Yorkshire Terrier, do not have a protective undercoat of 'downy' hair and as a result have sensitive skin that can easily be cut by rough brushing and combing, so proceed carefully.

The daily brushing should begin with a gentle teasing out of the tangles with a slicker brush, always remembering to be careful not to touch the skin. Owners should then go on to a bristle brushing and a final thorough comb-through with a wide-toothed comb.

Silky-coated dogs can accumulate a lot of dead hair, so they should be trimmed with scissors every three months or so. Electric clippering should be avoided because it fails to take out the dead hair.

BATHING

Opinions differ widely on the best policy towards bathing dogs. Some owners favour regular, monthly baths, while others don't bath their dogs fully at all. There is no definitive answer. Ultimately it is going to be a matter of personal choice, with the breed and coat type of the dog itself being an influence on that choice.

It is no surprise that many dogs intensely dislike having a bath. They don't like going against their instincts, and bathing does precisely that. In the wild, the wolf maintains its coat naturally. Each year they grow a good, warm coat in winter then lose this during the spring, when they moult. They help this shedding process along by rubbing up against stones and rocks, trees and gravel – anything they can find to scratch it off. They also dive into water to help rid themselves of the dead hair. During the rest of the year, their coat maintains itself thanks to the oil, or sebum, secreted by their bodies. It is a natural cycle.

The difference with the domestic dog, obviously, is that we expect it to blend in with our environment and the sanitary standards we set. We don't want dogs that smell or are in any way offensive. But, once again, we forget to look at this from the dog's point of view. To the dog its smell is an important way to blend in with its environment. If it smells of the natural world in the vicinity it is less conspicuous, and therefore less liable to attack. A dog knows that the more it smells of soap or shampoo, the less it blends in. And this is why a dog will protest when it is given a bath.

Many owners find that when they finish bathing their dog, it immediately runs off and rolls in something disgusting. When you finish your work it looks pristine but minutes later it looks as though it needs another bath. Dogs don't do this because they like to be dirty. Quite the opposite, in fact; they are naturally clean animals. The reason they do this is because the shampoo smell is not natural. They prefer to smell like their environment.

This can present something of a dilemma when it comes to bathing your dog. In general, it can help to bear in mind the following principles.

USE LOW- OR NON-PERFUMED SHAMPOOS
The more pungent the smell of the dog's coat when it dries out, the more likely it is to want to wash that smell away immediately. There are plenty of shampoos on the market that do not have a heavy aroma. Use them.

HOW TO GIVE YOUR PUPPY A BATH
It might be helpful to have a second pair of hands, to hold the dog steady during shampooing.

1. Begin by taking off the dog's collar and lifting it into the bath. If you can get bigger dogs in your bath fine, but if not bathe it outside with a bowl of clean, warm water.

2. With a shower or a pouring jug, wet the dog's back and work the water into its coat on the sides and at the back.

3. Apply the shampoo, working its way in throughout the body, legs, ears and head. Take care not to get soap in the dog's eyes. Keep a damp flannel to hand in case this should happen and be careful to wipe the eyes gently.

4. Rinse the dog thoroughly from the head backwards.

5. In warm weather, give the dog a good run afterwards to dry out. Longer-coated dogs may need towelling first. In cold weather, towel the dog down well and let it dry somewhere warm to prevent it catching cold. If you are using a hair dryer, introduce it gently and with care, as the dog may be scared by the noise.

DON'T OVERBATHE

If you do bathe your dog, don't overdo it. The dog's secretion of sebum maintains its coat. By washing too much this natural effect can be disrupted, causing problems. Thanks to human intervention, dogs have evolved a long way from their natural model. As a result, we have produced coats that require varying degrees of maintenance.

At one extreme, you have breeds like the American Cocker Spaniel. With its hair trailing to the ground it looks like a hovercraft and gathers dirt at a prodigious rate. If you don't bath it, or at least wash the trailing fur areas, on a regular basis – roughly monthly – you are going to have a lot of problems. At the other end of the scale are the short-coated dogs. This is nature's design, so if you have got a smooth-coated dog you don't need to wash it much more than once a year. If it rolls in something absolutely diabolical then just wash the affected area.

In between these two extremes you have breeds whose bathing requirements are dictated by their physical nature. Cocker Spaniels, for instance, need their ears washed on a regular basis. Boxers and Pugs need their eyes wiped a lot. A Sharpei needs to have all its wrinkles and folds wiped out regularly.

BRUSHING YOUR PUPPY'S TEETH

Maintaining a good, healthy set of teeth and gums is vital. Yellow, sticky plaque can build up on the surface of the teeth and, if it accumulates, it can form a cement-like, mineralised deposit called tartar. This in turn becomes a breeding ground for gum diseases that can, if left unchecked, produce bacteria that spread to the rest of the body and cause serious illness (see pages 144–5). Dogs are also prone to getting foreign objects stuck in their mouths and there are a number of conditions that can affect the exterior of the dog's mouth (see pages 146–7). So it is important that grooming includes a thorough cleaning and checking of these areas.

The key to good healthy teeth and gums is regular brushing. Chewing on bones and crunchy foods will help, but there is no alternative to using a toothbrush as the ultimate protection.

This, obviously, is something the dog isn't going to be able to do itself so you are going to have to do it on its behalf. It's another opportunity to build up the bond of trust between dog and owner and should be taken slowly and carefully at first. There are a few key things to remember.

- Start slowly, using a child's toothbrush and a little specially-formulated dog toothpaste.
- At first, brush the puppy's teeth only for a few seconds at a time each day, building it up over a period of days and weeks until it is happy to let you do it at any time. After that you can reduce the cleaning so that it conforms to a lifelong pattern in which you try to brush your dog's teeth once a month or so.

The earlier we get into the habit of checking and maintaining our dogs' teeth, the better.

CLAW CLIPPING

In the wild puppies keep their extremely sharp claws blunt by scratching in the soil. It is nature's way of protecting them – and their mother, who can easily be scratched and cut by the sharp nails within the claws. The domestic dog lives in artificial surroundings so this doesn't happen. To avoid puppies digging into their owners and hurting them, their claws need to be clipped when they grow too long. Here's how to do it.

- Place the puppy on a raised surface and, with one arm restraining it around the midriff, take each paw in turn.
- Every claw has a vein or 'quick' which will bleed profusely if you cut it, so great care must be taken to avoid doing this. When pups are small there is a clear whiteness to the tip of the nail. Using a pair of nail scissors or clippers, take a little bit of this off at a time until you see the vein coming through.
- If you allow the claw to grow longer then the quick will grow longer as well. Regular clipping during grooming will allow you to keep the quick back.
- If your puppy has darker claws it is more difficult to spot the vein. In this case, it is advisable to use a nail file to make the end of the claw blunt. Equally, periods of running around on concrete can also help dull the sharpness of the claws.
- Keep a little antiseptic or bandage at hand in case of accidents.

DEW CLAW

Dogs are born with the equivalent of a thumb on the sides of their front legs and very occasionally on their back ones too. This is known as a dew claw. It's a product of evolution, a part of the dog's anatomy that has – over generations – become obsolete. In some instances it may need to be removed, particularly if it is likely to grow inward and cause pain or, in the case of working dogs, if it is likely to get caught in undergrowth. In some breeds, the breed standard may require their removal. If it is required, a vet should do the job, preferably during the dog's first few days.

If the dew claws are to remain, however, they should be checked along with the rest of the foot during grooming. Any accumulation of hair, dirt or grease should be removed. The claw should be trimmed, like the rest of the claws, to avoid it growing inwards.

❧ ❧ ❧ ❧ ❧ ❧ ❧ ❧

Grooming provides the perfect opportunity to check on your dog's general condition, so be alert. You will not be able to give it as thorough an examination as a vet would do, but in chapter 9 there are descriptions of signs to watch out for that could indicate a problem with your puppy's health. If you are able to spot symptoms early on, you could avoid huge vets' bills and save your dog a lot of pain and discomfort. You could even save its life.

8 | BEHAVIOURAL PROBLEMS AND SOLUTIONS

There is no more wonderful sight than an exuberant young dog enjoying itself. Dogs at this age seem to have a boundless energy and they use every ounce of it, bouncing and bounding around, exploring every nook and crannie of their ever-expanding world. But there is a thin line between exuberance and bad behaviour, and many puppies will cross that line. During its first eight weeks the puppy was given the freedom to learn. It is now exploring and expanding its horizons, but it must learn where the boundaries are – and it is your job to teach it. In this chapter, some common behavioural problems are described, along with ways of dealing with them.

CHEWING

At around eight weeks old, puppies may start to chew furniture, upholstery or clothing. Of course, they don't know any better. They don't recognise the difference between a dishcloth and an expensive set of curtains. Both are potential playthings, as far as they are concerned, but this is plainly unacceptable behaviour and it must be tackled or it will escalate into serious misbehaviour when the dog gets older.

You should always bear in mind that the puppy is still going through teething. Its milk teeth are slowly being replaced by its adult teeth, which will need exercising. Adding some bone to the dog's diet will help enormously (see pages 66–7 for advice on the types of bone to choose).

Playtime presents the perfect medium through which to nip chewing habits in the bud.

If the dog is doing something undesirable, whether chewing a piece of furniture or digging its teeth into a sofa or a pair of curtains, produce the toy box and distract it by throwing a good, chewable toy. You are making a powerful statement about controlling the playtime, so this will not undermine your leadership.

Let the dog gnaw away at the toy for long enough to give its teeth a thorough workout – 10 to 15 minutes should do it. Then, when the dog's interest is waning, reclaim the toy. Make sure you don't get into a tugging contest as you do so. If the dog settles down, call it to you and reward it with some food. If the dog starts chewing at furniture again, you haven't given it enough time, so reintroduce the chewable toy.

See page 89 for advice on what to do if your puppy starts biting or nipping human beings.

INDEPENDENCE ANXIETY

Being removed from their litter can be a very traumatic experience for an eight-week-old dog. Their every instinct tells them they must stay within the safety of the pack and – so far, at least – that pack has been their canine family, their mother and the litter.

During its first days and weeks in a new home, a puppy can feel frightened and abandoned, and it may cry a lot. In reality the sound is more like a constant whining, but it is distressing nevertheless. And it must be dealt with decisively and quickly, before the anxiety worsens.

During the first 48 hours, you have compensated for the absence of its family by keeping it close to you, but now you have to teach the dog independence. You have to teach it that there will be times in its life when it will be alone. But you must also teach it that it is perfectly safe when that happens.

This can be hard for owners to do, especially if the dog is new to the home, but it is for the dog's own good. The worst possible thing you can do is say, 'Oh, it's a phase the dog will grow out of.' What will happen is that the dog will grow into the habit and the result will be serious separation anxiety as it matures.

Teaching a dog independence is something that is done gradually. You must let it get used to you being away for short periods at first, then for longer, more extended times.

The key steps are as follows.

1. Before you are going to leave the dog for a time, feed and toilet it first, then play with it for a short while. It will probably be ready for a sleep after this.
2. Put a radio on at low volume so that the room won't be plunged into complete silence when you go.
3. Bring the playtime to a close, leave the room and close the door or gate, ensuring the dog cannot follow you.
4. Stay away for between 10 and 30 minutes. At first remain in the house, using the time to do a household chore, take a bath or mow the lawn in the garden.

5. When you return, the dog will probably be overjoyed to see you but you must not make any fuss or bother. Don't interact with it for five minutes or so or until it has calmed down. Be careful not to make direct eye contact during this time.

6. When the five minutes have elapsed, play with the dog for a good ten minutes, cuddling it and generally making a fuss of it.

7. Repeat this process on a regular basis, slowly extending the period of time that you are separated from the dog.

This exercise will teach the dog some important lessons. Firstly, it will begin to learn that lengthy separations are a normal part of life. Secondly, it will see that these separations are nothing to be feared. Both lessons are vital if the dog is to be well-adjusted and to fit into the daily life of the home.

CRYING AT NIGHT

Dogs often cry at night during the settling-in phase. Again, it is hardly surprising. We go to sleep each night having locked the doors and shut the windows, happy that the house is secure. But what if we were to go to bed with the doors wide open. Would we sleep a wink?

This is the situation the dog faces each night as it goes to sleep in this new environment. It has no concept of what a lock is. As far as it is concerned, the house is vulnerable to any number of threats. And in the darkness of night, its fear of these potential threats is magnified many times over.

If your dog cries during the night you need to act decisively to let it know it is safe. Put on a light and check first that it does not want to go to the toilet. Do this in a very matter-of-fact way, by offering it the chance to go through the door. If it doesn't want to go to the toilet, you must signal your displeasure, but don't do it by scolding or raising your voice. Instead you must issue it with a disapproving look, the sort of stern look your mother used to give you when you were a child. The puppy will, more than likely, be standing there wagging its tail, looking pleadingly at you. But you must not fall for it. Switch the light off and return to bed.

This may well have to be repeated several times, but you have to remain strong. Eventually the dog will learn that it is not alone and therefore doesn't need to feel anxious about that. It must also learn that it is living by the human rules of the house and according to those human rules, nighttime is sleeping time. Most importantly, it will learn that it is safe and that the house's descent into darkness and quiet at night is nothing to be frightened of.

It can be a difficult step to achieve, but it is worth persevering for several reasons – not just so that you get a decent night's sleep. By establishing this precedent early on, you will have taught the dog to read your facial expressions. This will lay good groundwork for later. You will also have achieved the desired result without resorting to raising your voice, leaving this option open to you for another time and making it all the more powerful when you do choose to use it.

PERCEIVED DANGER

Some of the most extreme behaviour dogs demonstrate occurs in situations when something out of the ordinary happens within the household, such as a visitor arriving or someone knocking on the front door. Depending on their personalities, dogs can become aggressive in these situations.

It is not hard to understand why this is when you look at it from the dog's perspective. If it believes it is leader – which it will unless it has been given the correct information by its owner – the dog will regard the protection and security of the den as one of its absolute priorities. As leader, the buck stops with them. Therefore, the sound of the doorbell or the front knocker sets alarm bells ringing for the dog. And unless the person at the door is able to explain precisely who they are, why they are there and what they intend to do in the house, and do so in canine language, the dog is going to assume the worst, and as a result it is not going to be terribly well-disposed to the visitor.

Similarly, even the arrival of the morning post is a threat. How is a dog to know the strange paper objects being thrust through the letterbox aren't some sort of danger to it and the household? So is it any wonder it may attack the hand that is delivering this unknown menace into the house, given half a chance?

To add to the confusion the dog feels, at times the owners can exacerbate the situation. When they see their dog barking or leaping around manically at the sound of someone at the front door, it is all too easy for an owner to become embarrassed or angry and castigate the dog. In the worst cases owners can become physically abusive. This doesn't make any sense to the dog, who thinks it is fulfilling its role as the guardian of the household. It would expect the humans to congratulate it, not shout and remonstrate.

Given all this it is vital that, as they establish their relationship with the dog, owners learn to relieve their pet of their responsibility for dealing with these situations as soon as possible.

DEALING WITH TIMES OF PERCEIVED DANGER

The domestic home is a minefield of sights and sounds that could easily be construed as being potentially dangerous. Outside there is the sound of cars, lorries, aeroplanes and passersby. Inside there are the assorted sounds of daily life – from washing machines and telephones to the bumps and bangs of young children crashing around in their rooms. Dogs who believe they are in charge of the domestic pack can perceive all of these as a potential attack on the den and react accordingly.

The key to successfully managing perceived threats lies in displaying firm, decisive leadership. The dog must first be reminded of its status as a subordinate. It must then be reminded that this role does not require it to deal with the situation at hand. If it believes wholeheartedly in your ability to lead, your dog will trust you no matter what the perceived danger.

So whenever something happens that could be perceived as a threat, you must instantly establish that you are going to deal with the situation. When the doorbell rings, for example, head for the door, ensuring that the dog is between you and the entrance.

If the dog barks or growls, simply say 'thank you'. You are conveying three messages here. As leader, you are acknowledging:

- that you have heard its warning;
- that you are grateful for its contribution;
- and that you will now deal with the matter.

If the visitor comes into the house and the dog carries on its undesirable behaviour, you have two choices. Either you can hold the dog close to you without speaking until it stops, or you can remove it to another room.

The important thing to remember is that you should always do this calmly and quickly. And no matter how irritating the dog may be, you must not chastise or shout at it. You must never dramatise the situation. By remaining calm, you are displaying all the credentials of a leader.

Repeat the same process if the dog becomes excited when a visitor is leaving. Again, thank it for its contribution and then deal with the matter yourself. By taking charge of the comings and goings in the house like this, you will help the dog to feel good about itself.

Remember, even after it is demoted from the role of leader, the dog's instincts are geared towards integrating itself into a happy and successful domestic pack. It wants to feel useful, that it is contributing. By listening to the dog's views, then telling it that it has contributed to defending the den, you are reassuring the dog about its importance as a pack member. The dog will appreciate this.

Of course, all dogs have different personalities and some may react to perceived danger in more aggressive ways. If the dog has a tendency to aggression, it should be fitted with a collar during the early days of tackling its errant behaviour. If it leaps up or attacks a visitor, you must act decisively. The dog should be led by the collar or, if necessary, a lead, away from the visitor. The owner should then guide the visitor into the house and away from the dog. If the dog fails to remain out of the way, the owner must remove it from the scene. This way it will begin to learn the consequences of its actions.

ANIMAL RIVALRIES

Many people have problems integrating new dogs into a home that already has one or more dogs living there. This is no surprise. The human members of the domestic 'pack' should be higher in status than the dogs, and below this there will also be a canine pecking order. Sometimes this will establish itself simply, without any confrontation, but dogs can be hugely competitive and a power struggle may result in aggressive and potentially violent behaviour. This is why it is best if the new dog is introduced to its housemate or mates beforehand, on neutral territory. In an ideal world, more than one meeting would be beneficial. Reputable breeders should allow this, and they should also be happy to keep the puppy until it is ready to integrate with its new companions. In the unlikely event that the dogs form a dangerous dislike for each other, the breeder should agree to keep their dog without a second thought.

Unfortunately, we live in a less than ideal world, and if you find there is a power struggle going on, you should keep the dogs in question separated whenever you are not there to supervise their behaviour until the situation is resolved.

A dog doesn't make any assumptions about what sort of pack it is going to live within. It lives with whatever is sharing its space, whether that is humans, other dogs – or indeed other species. In general, it assimilates well into any environment. Owners can experience problems in integrating their dog with other species, however. This situation needs careful handling.

If a dog has difficulty settling into the home with another animal, such as a cat or a rabbit, you should slip a lead on the dog whenever it is in the same space. If it makes any sort of move towards the other animal, you will be able to restrain it easily. The important thing is that you don't turn this into a huge drama. Don't shout or scold. Just ignore it. After a while the dog's agitation or excitement will ease.

Smaller animals may present more of a challenge, long term. You should remember that the dog remains a predator. For this reason, it should not be left on its own with smaller animals, such as hamsters or chickens, at any time. And, of course, never leave dogs unattended with babies or small children.

TOILET TROUBLES

Most dogs journey through life without too many toilet troubles because their natural instincts tell them they should remain clean and perform their bodily functions in an outdoor environment. An owner's job should be to work with this nature, to lead them to the correct routine and to reward them when they get there.

Life, of course, isn't always as straightforward as this, and some dogs have problems with toilet training. Part of the blame for this may lie with the owner or breeder for not having trained the dog during the crucial three- to eight-week period when it begins to go to the toilet on its own. But the more serious problems are rooted in the dog's mistaken sense of its place within the pack. If a dog believes it is leader and is responsible, it will become anxious and nervous. This in turn can cause it to mark out its territory or lose control of its functions, hence the bedwetting or involuntary urination and diarrhoea. This downward spiral can accelerate, especially if the dog's owners react dramatically or scold when it does its toileting. This simply worsens the situation. The dog believes its job is to make the pack happy. If its toileting is doing the opposite and making its human charges distinctly unhappy, it will try to circumvent this by disposing of the evidence. The most common manifestations of toilet troubles are:

- unpredictable defecating round the home;
- eating up of faeces when doing so;
- diarrhoea;
- and wetting itself.

TREATING TOILET TROUBLES

Toilet troubles can be very upsetting for all concerned. It goes without saying that having a dog defecate on a clean carpet or sofa is deeply unpleasant. Yet the key to curing this problem lies in masking these feelings.

If a dog is defecating and/or urinating at random around the house, the first thing to do is remove it from its perceived role as leader. Once it is relieved of the notion that it is in charge, it will be relieved of the anxiety it feels about being in charge.

Monitor your dog's toilet habits. First thing in the morning and at mealtimes, look for telltale signs of toileting, such as circling. When you see this, give the dog the opportunity to go to the correct spot, by opening the door to the garden, for instance. If the dog does defecate or urinate somewhere it shouldn't, don't get angry; just clear it up and carry on as if nothing has happened. The worst thing an owner can do is make a song and dance about it.

If, on the other hand, the dog urinates or defecates in the right spot, then it should be rewarded with food and praised for being a 'good dog' or a 'clean dog'. This will help to renew its good association with the right spot. With patience and calm, it will soon begin using this spot all the time again.

If your dog has been eating its faeces, you need to distract it and draw it away after its toileting. The best way to do this is when it has defecated in the allocated spot, call it to you with a food reward, praise it by saying 'clean dog' then remove it into the house. While the dog is inside, happy and focused on its treat, you can remove and dispose of the faeces quickly and without any fuss.

Additionally, by adding pineapple or courgette to the dog's diet, you will reduce its tendency to eat its faeces. For some reason, both make it unpalatable.

Above all, with patience, vigilance and, above all, calmness, the problem should soon be alleviated.

OVER-AMOROUS BEHAVIOUR

By the age of five months, male dogs will be able to produce sperm and by the age of six months a female may be ready to have her first season (for more on this, see pages 189–91). Dogs can become over-amorous around puberty. Their hormones are flying all over the place and they may try to simulate sex with each other. It is not just confined to males; bitches too can climb on top of each other or onto toys or pieces of furniture, even their blankets. It is, of course, perfectly natural, but because it doesn't fit in with what we expect to see in our human world and embarrasses owners, it is to be discouraged.

Rather than rushing to have the dog neutered (see pages 191–3), there is a straightforward way to deal with this. The dog must simply be taught its behaviour is not acceptable.

1. Take hold of the dog's collar gently but firmly without saying anything.
2. Remove it from the other dog or the object in question.

3. Hold it while it remains excited, again making sure to be firm but not aggressive. Do not speak as you do so or you will block their learning process.
4. When the dog's body has relaxed, let it go. If it returns to the dog or the object of its attention, repeat the process.

❀ ❀ ❀ ❀ ❀ ❀ ❀

You may experience other variations on the behavioural problems described in this chapter, but the solutions all follow the same principles. Make sure the dog understands clearly that you are in control, as pack leader. Make sure it knows that you will protect it from harm. Don't over-react to bad behaviour; if necessary remove the dog from the situation, but do it without shouting or scolding. And keep forming positive associations by praising and rewarding good behaviour. Your dog will get the message in the end!

9 | HEALTH CHECKS IN THE EARLY WEEKS

Keeping your dog fit and healthy is, perhaps, the most important duty you face as a new owner.

No matter how safe, clean and happy an environment you provide, your puppy faces a whole range of diseases and infestations, some of which can be life-threatening. The best way to deal with these is by prevention, through early worming, vaccinations, eye tests, good dental care and grooming. The earlier you begin practising each of these the better, if you are to avoid your puppy picking up a potentially serious illness.

VACCINATIONS

During the first few weeks of life, young puppies get immunity from disease from the colostrum in their mother's first milk. This immunity fades quite quickly, however; vets reckon it halves every eight days so that by the time a dog is between six and 12 weeks old it has faded altogether.

Dogs face a wide range of potential diseases, but there are five key viruses that present the greatest threat, particularly to the young dog. Prevention is the best form of cure and it is important that the puppy is vaccinated against these five main threats at some stage during the first six to ten weeks of life.

DISTEMPER OR 'HARD PAD'

One of the most dangerous diseases, this is more commonly known as 'hard pad' because it makes the pad of a dog's foot become hard, thickened and cracked. The distemper virus affects young dogs in urban and city areas in particular, and is passed on through urine, faeces and saliva. It can even be picked up by the dog inhaling tiny droplets of the virus that have been released into the air by a carrier's breath.

Distemper affects the dog's skin, eyes, nose, lungs, stomach and intestines, and results in a sore discharge from the eyes and nose. It can also lead to pneumonia, diarrhoea, vomiting and dehydration. Around half all dogs affected by it suffer fits.

Any signs of distemper require immediate treatment by a vet, as it is usually fatal.

HEPATITIS

A disease that initially attacks the liver, this is a particular danger to young dogs, especially those under the age of two. Like distemper, it is transmitted via faeces, saliva, urine and droplets breathed in from the air.

Hepatitis spreads to the liver via the bloodstream. It then destroys liver cells, causing the liver to become enlarged and inflamed. The results are jaundice, or yellowing, severe abdominal pain, vomiting, diarrhoea and dehydration. The virus can also damage the eyes and kidneys. In severe cases, hepatitis can kill a dog within 24 hours.

Owners of dogs that contract hepatitis and recover should be aware that their dogs will remain dangerous carriers for up to nine months afterwards and can pass on the disease via their urine.

PARVOVIRUS

Parvovirus is transmitted mainly through dog-to-dog contact and via faeces. It attacks the stomach and is a particular threat to puppies, who can also suffer inflammation of the heart. It's a particular menace because it is extremely resistant, surviving in the environment for a year or more and withstanding many types of disinfectant.

Parvovirus varies in its seriousness. Some dogs will experience vomiting, bloody diarrhoea, high temperature and dehydration, but nothing more severe. Others, however, can suffer depression and physical collapse. Some die, occasionally within 24 hours.

LEPTOSPIROSIS

A bacterial infection that can cause serious, even fatal, illness in humans, leptospirosis damages the liver, kidneys and blood vessels. It is passed by direct dog-to-dog contact, most commonly through urine, but also through cuts and grazes on the dog's feet.

Dogs infected by the virus suffer jaundice, haemorrhage, vomiting, black diarrhoea and severe dehydration. If the liver becomes enlarged it causes extreme abdominal pain. Damage to the kidneys can, in the worst cases, precipitate kidney failure. Leptospirosis is not as resilient as parvovirus, however, and can be eliminated by disinfectants.

The severity of this disease can vary, but in the worst cases death can occur within two days.

KENNEL COUGH

In many senses, kennel cough is similar to human flu. It is highly infectious and is transmitted from dog to dog in highly populated environments such as kennels, puppy classes or dog shows. Like the other main diseases, it is transmitted through the air and breathed in. It then incubates for ten days or so. The first visible symptoms of the illness are sneezing, a dry cough and a loss of appetite.

The good news, however, is that – like human flu – it is very rarely fatal. Kennel cough tends to last for two to three weeks. However, owners must keep their dogs isolated afterwards because the illness can still be spread for up to ten weeks after the symptoms have cleared.

WHEN TO VACCINATE?

Opinion differs on when precisely the puppy's immunity should be topped up through vaccination. Some dog owners vaccinate against the five main diseases as early as six or seven weeks old. Others wait until ten weeks. It is pretty much accepted by all the experts that the latest vaccinations should be given is at 12 weeks old.

The reality is that it is dependent on what is going to happen to the dog in its first weeks and months. If it is going to travel with you on holiday, for instance, or if it is going to be crossing areas where other dogs walk freely, then the risk of picking up viruses is high and the puppy should be vaccinated early. If, on the other hand, the puppy is remaining at home with you and its litter then the need is not so pressing. As ever, if there is any doubt about the necessity of vaccinations, consult your vet.

WHY VACCINATE?

A lot of owners question the need to vaccinate their dog. The best answer to that is the low incidence of the main life-threatening diseases in this country today. The fact that killer diseases such as distemper and parvovirus are so rare is almost entirely because of the vaccination system. The other major point owners need to remember is that, unlike human diseases, the major dog diseases have no specific cures. If your dog contracts one of them it is, in all probability, going to die. Faced with that stark fact, no responsible owner thinks twice about vaccinating.

BOOSTERS

There is no certainty about how long the immunity the standard vaccination provides. It is a subject of great debate amongst vets. Some recommend annual boosters, while others advise that they are renewed every three years. Different owners are going to have different views on when – or indeed if – to give their dogs booster injections. It is compulsory, however, that dogs have a current certificate proving they are 'up to date' with their injections before travelling abroad or going into boarding kennels. If you are going to get a pet passport then you will need to get your dog micro-chipped so that it's vaccination and other medical details are recorded.

WORMING

Worms are an unfortunate fact of life. All dogs will have them at some point and most will have them during puppyhood, when they are most vulnerable. Worm infestation can cause weight loss, vomiting, diarrhoea and a painfully swollen abdomen. In the worst cases it can even cause death. So it's important that dogs are treated – or wormed – from an early age.

There are four main types of worms, each of which live in the dog's intestine and feed on undigested food there.

ROUNDWORMS

Roundworms are the most common worms in puppies; indeed, almost every puppy is born with them present. They look a little like a rubber band and can be several inches long. They are spread through the environment and other dogs' faeces.

Roundworms mainly infest the small intestine, but they can also affect the large intestine, blood vessels and respiratory tract. Roundworms can penetrate the wall of a puppy's gut and pass via the bloodstream into organs such as the liver and lungs. This in turn can lead to pneumonia, hepatitis and fits – all very serious problems.

TAPEWORMS

Of the several types of tapeworm that affect dogs, the most common lives in the small intestine, where it attaches its head to the lining and adds new sections to its body as it grows. By the time it is visible to the human eye, it resembles a string of white grains of rice joined together. Tapeworms are much rarer in puppies, turning up more commonly in adult dogs, and they are spread by fleas, which act as a host to the larvae during their early development. The most obvious sign of tapeworm infestation is a tickling in the anus region, which makes the dog drag or 'scoot' its bottom along the floor. The worms will be easily detectable either in the dog's faeces or protruding from its anus.

HOOKWORMS

Less common than roundworms, these parasites feed on the dog's blood and can cause anaemia. They are transmitted via larvae that hatch on moist ground from eggs passed in a dog's faeces.

Dogs can pick up the worms directly by ingesting the larvae accidentally from soil or grass. They are then passed on to puppies through their mother's milk or placenta. Hookworms can also infest the meat of other animals and transfer to dogs through their food. Hookworms are relatively easy to diagnose because they can ordinarily be seen by the naked eye.

WHIPWORMS

These thread-like parasites are around 5 to 7 centimetres long and live in the colon and small intestine. They are transmitted via eggs that have infested a dog's faeces and can only be passed on if the dogs ingest them directly. These, too, are bloodsuckers and, if present in large numbers, can cause bloody diarrhoea and lead to significant weight loss. In general, however, whipworms do not produce many eggs, which make them among the trickier types of worm to detect – even by a vet.

WHEN AND HOW TO WORM

Worms can be passed from the mother either before birth or through her milk, so it's crucial a breeder starts early, ideally when the puppy is two to three weeks old. Always check that the person who provides you with your puppy has begun this process. After that your dog should be wormed at least three times a year, throughout its life.

The good news is that all worms are relatively easy to eliminate. Thanks to the wide range of modern treatments available at vets' surgeries, owners have a wide range of options. Deworming medicines now come in tablets, granules or liquids. The liquid medicines have the advantage that you can administer them via a syringe, which can be used to squirt the medicine directly into the dog's mouth.

EYE TESTING

At some stage before it reaches the age of 12 weeks you will need to arrange for your dog to have a formal eye test. Eye abnormalities are common; in fact, most breeds are afflicted with them to a greater or lesser extent.

The most dangerous diseases are those that are inherited, not just because they can affect a dog early in its life but also because an unscrupulous or unthinking owner can spread them still further by breeding. As with other inherited conditions, such as hip dysplasia, the responsible authorities – in the case of the UK, the Kennel Club and the British Veterinary Association – have introduced eye tests that will identify whether or not a dog is a carrier of an eye disease. By getting owners to register the results of these tests they hope to reduce or even eradicate the problem. Responsible owners will not breed from dogs liable to pass on any of these diseases.

YOUR DOG'S FIRST EYE TEST

This should be carried out for the first time before the dog reaches 12 weeks of age, and then repeated once a year for the rest of the dog's life. Your vet should have a list of the 40 or so BVA panellists throughout the country. When you go to the appointment, you will need to take the dog's registration documents with you so the certificate of eye examination results can be added to them.

At the test, drops are put into the dog's eyes, which make the pupils large enough for the tester to see all the structures within. The dog will be examined for all inherited and acquired abnormalities within the eyeball and the associated structures, including the eyelids. The size and positioning of the eyes is also recorded. The dog will then be classified in one of three categories: clear, which is self explanatory; carrier, indicating they have an inherited condition; or affected, indicating they have an eye disorder present.

The results provide responsible owners and breeders with very simple advice for the future. Dogs which are affected should not breed. Nor, in general, should those that are shown to be carriers of inherited diseases. Only dogs pronounced clear should be viewed as potential breeding animals.

The most common inherited diseases of the eye, eyelids and eyelashes are as follows.

ENTROPION

The most common kind of eye disorder, this occurs when the eyelid turns inwards and the lashes dig into the eye as a result. It can cause tremendous irritation and ultimately lead to blindness. It is usually evident at birth when the pup's eyes open, but can develop later in life as well.

ECTROPION

Here the eyelid turns out and tears gather in the pouch formed as a result. This in turn causes the cornea to dry out. It can cause severe pain and, if left untreated, blindness.

TRICHIASIS

Here the eyelashes grow naturally in the wrong direction, rubbing directly on to the eyes. This causes redness and pain and – again – can cause severe ocular problems.

DISTICHIASIS

In this condition extra unwanted hairs grow on the edge of the eyelid rubbing on the eye.

THIRD EYELID OR 'CHERRY EYE'

Every dog has a third eyelid, otherwise known as the nictitating membrane. It acts a bit like a windscreen wiper, cleaning and lubricating the eye. In some breeds, such as the St Bernards and Bloodhound, it appears naturally, but in other breeds it is a sign of a problem, such as a rolled cartilage or a prolapsed nictitans gland. The telltale signs of a problem are a white membrane or a red, pea-shaped lump appearing in the inner corner of the eye – hence its other name, 'cherry eye'.

CONJUNCTIVITIS

As in humans, this is a painful condition caused when the dog's conjunctiva get inflamed. And as in humans, it can be caused by a variety of factors – from dust and smoke to a scratch or an infection. The most obvious signs of conjunctivitis are a redness in the eyes, or the dog screwing up its eyes or shedding tears.

GLAUCOMA

To function properly the eye needs a constant supply of fluid. If, however, the eye's drainage outlets become blocked, there can be a build-up of this fluid. This makes the ball of the eye stretch, building pressure on it. Telltale signs of glaucoma are redness, cloudiness, excessive tearing, eyeball swelling, pain, and sensitivity to light. Glaucoma can be treated by reducing the amount of fluid produced, improving the drainage or laser surgery.

CATARACTS

Cataracts affect the lens inside the eye, causing it to lose its transparency and become opaque in the affected area. The severity of the problem will depend on how much of the eye is affected: the opaqueness may affect the whole eye or a small area only. A small, non-progressive cataract will not impair the dog's vision too much. A complete cataract, on the other hand, will make it blind in the affected eye. Cataracts can occur in puppies if their mother has been ill or poorly fed during pregnancy.

KERATOCONJUNCTIVITIS SICCA (KCS)
OR 'DRY EYE'

'Dry eye' is a condition caused by the dog failing to produce the normal amount of tears. Tears clean and lubricate the surface of the eye, the cornea, and play an important role in controlling infection. Lack of tears can lead to chronic irritation of the cornea and conjunctiva, and can result in corneal ulcers and even blindness.

Dry eye can be caused by viral infections and inflammations. Breeds prone to it are the Bull Terrier, Cocker Spaniel, Lhasa Apso, Miniature Poodle, Miniature Schnauzer, Pekingese, Pug, Shih Tzu, Standard Schnauzer, West Highland White Terrier and Yorkshire Terrier.

The standard treatment for dry eye is to lubricate the eye regularly and to use stimulants that will produce tears.

PROGRESSIVE RETINAL ATROPHY (PRA)

The most serious disease affecting the retina is progressive retinal atrophy. This causes the blood supply to the retina to wither away slowly so that its light-sensitive cells die. An inherited and untreatable problem, it can often be hard to detect because it develops gradually. The first sign may come towards the end of the disease's development when the dog loses its night vision or – at worst – becomes totally blind.

COLLIE EYE ANOMALY (CEA)

Collie eye anomaly is almost exclusively confined to Collies and Shetland Sheepdogs. The illness develops deep inside the eye and can lead to the retina haemorrhaging or detaching itself, both of which cause blindness. A degree of CEA is present in a disturbingly large number of collies, although only one in 20 or so lose their sight because of it.

❀ ❀ ❀ ❀ ❀ ❀ ❀

This chapter has covered the medical procedures and tests all puppies need in their first 12 weeks. In the next chapter, I'll look at some of the other common health problems your dog might suffer from – and explain how to spot them and what to do about them.

10 | THE HOME VET: CHECKING YOUR DOG'S HEALTH

A diligent owner can often pick up illnesses or disorders at a very early stage, thus ensuring they are nipped in the bud. You might spot some symptoms while grooming your dog, or it could be that it loses its appetite and appears unwell. These are the key areas an owner should look at, along with advice on treating any problems that arise.

SKIN DISORDERS

A dog can be afflicted by a large number of skin problems, some of which can lead to serious diseases. They can be caused by everything from parasites, such as fleas, mites, lice and ticks, to infections. They can also be caused by dietary or hormonal problems, household cleaning products and hereditary conditions.

Invariably the problem, whatever it is, is made worse by the dog scratching itself. This in turn results in hair loss and inflammation, which leads to more scratching, and so on. It becomes a vicious circle, and can leave the dog permanently scarred.

No owner is going to recognise all of these potential problems, but by looking out for a few of the telltale signs, you can generally detect that something is amiss and act promptly. Often the best cure is simply to get the dog to stop scratching, either by the use of anti-inflammatory drugs or, if necessary, sedatives. But in some cases, the problem is a behavioural one, and needs to be treated on a more holistic level.

Signs of potential skin problems include the following.

HAIR LOSS

Watch out for areas of baldness, periods of prolonged moulting and broken hairs on the coat. The causes of these can range from excessive scratching, to dietary and hormonal imbalances. Dietary imbalances may be treatable at home with multivitamins and a little extra cod liver or vegetable oil in the dog's diet, but if in doubt consult the vet.

EXCESSIVE SCRATCHING

This is the most obvious sign of a problem, although, given the number of possible causes, the solution is usually far less obvious. The first thing to do is to look at the area where the dog is concentrating its attention. If, for instance, it is scratching at sores around the base of its tail, the problem may be impacted anal sacs (see page 149). Otherwise look for any parasites or spots, sores or inflamed areas of the skin. Many parasites can be treated at home with special treatments (see pages 134–8). Sores or signs of bacterial infection, however, should be treated by a vet.

REDDENING OF THE SKIN

Again there are myriad explanations for this, from fleas, lice, ringworm and bacterial sores to different forms of dermatitis. If the irritated area is relatively small and localised, it can be treated by applying calamine lotion. If it is more widespread, it can be alleviated by washing the dog in a lanolin baby shampoo and applying flea spray when it is dry. As ever, though, if the problem persists, consult the vet.

RASHES

Look for itchy red spots on the ears, elbows and hocks. The usual cause of this is sarcoptic mange, more commonly known as scabies, a very nasty condition that can affect humans who come into contact with it as well (see page 137). Other signs to look out for are areas wet from licking, dandruff, matted coats, and dry or scaly skin.

EXTERNAL PARASITES

It's a fact of life that your dog will probably be affected by an external parasite at some point in its life. At an early age, even before you have taken it out for its first walk, it is important to look out for the main nuisances: fleas, ticks, lice and mites.

FLEAS

A flea's life cycle is divided into four stages – egg, larva, pupa and adult. The whole process from egg to flea can take as little as two weeks. An adult flea lives for no more than seven or ten days, but during this time it causes immense discomfort to a 'host' dog.

When fleas move through a dog's coat, they cause huge irritation and the dog will begin scratching, biting or licking at the area where the itching is concentrated. In some cases, dogs will be allergic to the bites of the flea and display pronounced skin problems even though there is no obvious indication of fleas being present.

Fleas are hard to spot: they are small and difficult for the naked eye to pick up, and they also move around the body quickly. Fleas do, however, tend to settle in the same regions of the dog's body, usually around the base of the tail, the ears, neck and abdomen. One simple way of checking whether they are present is by combing through the dog's coat and shaking any loose matter on to a small piece of white tissue paper. If there are flecks of red, this is probably ingested blood from an infestation of fleas.

How to treat fleas
Left untreated, fleas can cause widespread problems, such as anaemia. They can also multiply at a terrifying rate and infest an entire household, including all the human occupants. So it is important to treat fleas – and do so quickly.

There are a variety of flea controls, ranging from flea collars and powders to shampoos and sprays. It used to be that you had to dust the dog's entire body but, thanks to modern medicine, single 'spot on' treatments can now be applied to the back of the neck. The treatment spreads from there, giving good protection to the whole of the body. Depending on where your dog is sleeping, you might want to consider washing bedding, cushion covers etc.

Fleas are also host to tapeworms, so if they are present, it is vital that you worm the dog as well (see pages 123–5).

TICKS

Ticks are unpleasant, blood-sucking parasites that can afflict dogs everywhere. The most common varieties are the sheep and hedgehog ticks, which – as their names suggest – originate in other species then cross over to dogs as they roam in grass, woodland or overgrowth. Ticks are generally less common than fleas, but they can cause abscesses and infections. In some parts of the world, they can transmit potentially lethal diseases, such as Lyme disease. It is vital, therefore, that they are treated quickly and effectively.

The life cycle of a tick is thought to last up to three years and consists of three phases, but it is the final one that causes the damage, when the fully-grown tick finds the point of least resistance in a dog's coat and fixes itself on by its mouth. Often this is the face, the ears or the abdomen. It then begins to feed on the dog's blood supply, passing on any infections it is carrying at the same time. Because it burrows into the skin it can leave nasty abscesses.

The most obvious sign of ticks is a small, grey dot on the dog's skin. It is easy to mistake the dot for a wart or another lump, but the most obvious sign that it is a tick is that it will grow larger, often to the size of a pea.

How to treat ticks

Removing the tick can be a tricky process because it attaches itself to the dog's skin by its mouth. It is easy to remove the body but leave the mouth attached, which can lead to more severe problems. If ticks do appear on your puppy you should see your vet as they can cause anaemia and, occasionally, death. Ticks can also transmit infectious diseases to humans so it is important to act quickly.

You can treat your dogs in advance for ticks with an over-the-counter treatment. If you live in a rural area and plan to walk your dog in open fields or woodland it is advisable to do this. It should always be treated if it is likely to come into contact with sheep.

MITES

There are three types of mite that can cause problems for puppies.

'Juvenile pyoderma' is a particularly nasty problem in puppies, caused by their lack of natural defences against demodex, one of the most common mites. Most dogs carry this mite without any problems, but it can cause nasty dermatitis around the head and shoulders of puppies which, if infected, can lead to pyoderma. Dobermans, Dachshunds and Irish Setters are particularly prone to this condition, which can also be spotted by the 'mousy' odour that it produces. See a vet if you spot any of the telltale signs, such as areas of hair loss, scaley skin, oozing abscesses and ulceration.

Scabies is caused by sarcoptic mites burrowing into the dog's skin and laying eggs in the resultant tunnels. The itching caused by this can be very intense and the dog can scar itself badly with scratching. Scabies is best treated by insecticidal shampoo, but sedative drugs may also be needed to prevent the dog mutilating itself.

The otodectes mite is the only one visible to the naked eye. It causes inflammation of the ear and can be seen in the shape of tiny white moving dots inside the canal of the ear. Once again, see your vet to confirm the diagnosis and get treatment.

EAR DISORDERS

Ear infections are relatively common in dogs and take two main forms – infections of the external ear canal, known as otitis externa, and infections of the middle ear, or otitis media. Some breeds are more prone than others to infection. Dogs with floppy ears, such as Cocker Spaniels or Basset Hounds, are vulnerable because of the lack of ventilation that gets into the ear canal. This in turn can lead to overheating, which can lead to any excess wax inside the ear becoming infected. Dogs with very tight, curly coats, such as Poodles and Schnauzers, suffer because they have narrow ear canals, which can lead to an accumulation of hair and wax and create a breeding ground for infections.

There are three telltale signs of a problem with a dog's ears. The first two should be detectable during your regular inspection of the dog.

DISCHARGES FROM THE EAR

There are three main types of discharge, each indicating an infection of the outer ear, otitis externa:

- If the discharge is gritty and flecked with dark material, the most likely cause is ear mites.
- If the discharge is runny and dark, this suggests it is caused by a yeast infection.

🐾 If the discharge is thick and yellow, this suggests a bacterial infection.

In all these cases, consult your vet.

SWOLLEN OR PAINFUL EARS

If you see your dog shaking its head, twitching or pawing at its ears, or if it registers discomfort or flinching when you touch it around the ear area, there are a number of possible causes:

🐾 If there is a swelling on the inside of the ear flap, the most likely cause is an aural haematoma.

🐾 If the ear looks clean but the dog still seems distressed when it is touched, this suggests a foreign object, such as a grass seed may have become lodged in the ear. As with humans, it's inadvisable to put anything in a dog's ear, so avoid trying to dislodge this yourself and consult a vet.

POOR HEARING

It's rare for dogs to go completely deaf, but infections of the ear can temporarily impair their hearing. There are a few telltale signs that a dog has got a problem with its hearing:

🐾 It tilts or scratches at its head.

🐾 It fails to respond as normal when called for its walk or meals.

🐾 There is a discharge from the ear (see above).

HOW TO CHECK YOUR DOG'S EARS

Look into the ear canal by lifting the ear flap. Use a torch if necessary. The inside of the canal should be clean, much like the skin on the hairless section of the belly. The main things to look out for are inflammations and excesses of hair and wax. A small amount of wax is not a worry and can be left alone, but if there is a build-up of wax plugging the canal it must be cleaned. Similarly, clogging by dead hairs must also be cleaned. Do this by putting some cotton wool over the tip of your finger. Be careful not to prod around too much and avoid using cotton buds, which can do damage. Finish off by applying an ear-cleaning liquid of the kind generally available at vets' surgeries. Place a few drops inside the ear then clean around the outer surface of the ear with cotton wool.

It's also important to smell the ear for unpleasant odours, which are a good indicator of infections. Any cause for concern should be reported to the vet.

EYE PROBLEMS

A dog's eyes are vulnerable to a wide range of diseases and disorders. Some of these are inherited, others develop later in life, while yet more are caused by injury or infection. A puppy should have a formal eye test at some point before it reaches the age of 12 weeks to check for any permanent conditions or inherited diseases (see pages 126–30).

Even before this, however, your physical check-up of your dog during grooming may show up some of the tell-tale signs of eye problems.

Obviously, if your dog starts displaying signs of impaired vision, such as bumping into furniture or walking more slowly and carefully than normal, you should hear alarm bells and head to the vet immediately. Some other signs to watch out for are as follows.

SLEEPY EYES

Many dogs get small deposits of 'sleep' or mucus that gathers in the corner of the eye. It is not in itself threatening but if left to dry it can be a magnet for infection and bacteria. Use grooming as an opportunity to either pick out the 'sleep' with a finger or, if it has begun to dry, use a wet ball of cotton wool to clean the mucus away.

SWOLLEN EYES

There are two primary types of swelling that can affect a dog's eyes. The tissues behind the eye can become inflamed and can swell, pushing the eye forward, or the eyeball itself can grow so that it is forced out of its socket. The most obvious signs of a problem of this kind are problems with closing the eyelids, dilated pupils, a glazed expression in the eyes and one eyeball protruding more than another. Always consult your vet if these occur.

WEEPING EYES

A variety of discharges, or epiphora, can indicate eye disorders or diseases.

- ❧ If the discharge is clear, it suggests the dog may have conjunctivitis, in the worst case, or, in less serious instances, a blocked tear duct.
- ❧ If the discharge is cloudy or discoloured and thick, it suggests there is an infection, such as distemper (see page 119).

You can help avoid both by careful clipping of the hair around the eyes. In the short term they can be alleviated by irrigating the eye with an eyewash, a boracic acid solution or cold weak tea. In the long term, however, if the problem persists, you should consult your vet.

YOUR DOG'S TEETH

It is not overstating things to say that in the wild strong and healthy teeth are the most vital weapon a wolf can possess. Its survival depends on them. It is with its teeth that a wolf captures its prey. It is with its teeth that it kills, dismembers and divides up its food.

These functions also maintain the wolf's dental health. By ripping, gnawing and chewing at carcasses – often for long periods of time – the wolf simultaneously maintains the sharpness of its teeth, massages its gums and releases increased amounts of healthy saliva into its mouth. The extensive work-out it gives its teeth on an almost daily basis prevents the build-up of damaging tartar and also staves off gum diseases.

Of course, these natural processes are not available to our domestic animals. The sometimes woeful state of our dogs' teeth is underlined by recent statistics which indicate that some 85 per cent of dogs suffer from dental problems. By far the most common complaints are excessive build-ups of tartar and gum diseases, specifically gingivitis. Our dogs' dental health is one of those areas that is often relegated to the bottom of owners' list of tasks to deal with, yet it is one of the most vital aspects of all.

Thankfully, the better dog food manufacturers have developed special teeth-friendly foods that release minerals, which become embedded in the plaque of the teeth and block the build-up of tartar. They make these foods in the form of a crunchy kibble, which gives the dog something substantial to chew on. They are not quite the equivalent of a wolf working its way through its prey – kibble often doesn't give the incisors or canines at the front of the mouth the stimulation they need – so the dog's teeth will still need to be brushed as well. As the dog gets older we can give them bones to gnaw during playtime.

CHECKING YOUR PUPPY'S MOUTH
It is important this is done gently and carefully once the bond of trust is established.

1. Sit the dog on a raised surface, so that you can see its mouth from every angle.
2. Firmly hold the lower jaw with one hand then, with the other hand, draw down the lower lip and raise the upper lip to reveal the teeth and gums.

3. Firstly examine the outsides of the teeth, looking for discolouration or a lack of the usual, healthy translucence a healthy tooth has. If there is discolouration, it may indicate dead tooth pulp.

4. Look for obvious build-ups of mineral-like tartar, the forerunner to gum disease.

5. Examine the gums on both sides of the jaw for any signs of inflammation or discolouration.

6. To look at the upper jaw, use your thumb and forefinger to open the mouth further.

7. Inspect not just the inner teeth and gums but also the hard palate and the tongue.

8. Finally, smell the dog's breath. If it smells unpleasant, consult your vet.

The main dental disorders are listed below, along with advice on how to treat them yourself and when to consult a vet.

HALITOSIS

Bad breath is usually caused by one of three things: bacteria developing in the debris trapped between the teeth, tartar or a gum infection. Any hint of it should be reported to the vet.

GUM DISEASES

There are two main gum conditions, both relating to the tissue surrounding the teeth. Gingivitis is an inflammation that develops in the gums, or gingiva, when bacteria accumulates. Periodontal disease occurs in the periodontal ligament, the deeper structure around the tooth. This is very common in dogs; indeed, almost every dog will develop it at some period in their life. There are specially formulated toothpastes and antiseptic mouthwashes that can help combat infections at an early stage but if these don't work within a day or so, see your vet.

RETAINED BABY TEETH

At around the five-month mark, the baby teeth are replaced by the adult teeth (see pages 188–9). At this point the deciduous teeth normally fall out and are often reabsorbed by the dog. In some cases, however, a few baby teeth remain in place and when the adult teeth come up alongside them, they are pushed out of their normal alignment. This can lead to severe problems for the dog and needs to be dealt with early. Once the adult teeth start coming through, the dog's jaw should be checked regularly for signs of double sets of teeth. If it happens, the baby teeth will need to be extracted.

MALOCCLUSIONS

The 'perfect' canine bite, or occlusion, occurs when the jaw closes and the upper incisors just overlap the lower ones. Jaws that deviate from this norm are known as malocclusions. A jaw in which the lower jaw is much shorter than the upper jaw is known as an overshot jaw. The reverse, in which the lower jaw is longer than the upper one, is known as an undershot jaw. Because of selective breeding, these conditions are now common in around 20 per cent of dogs. The Boxer, for instance, has been bred specifically to have an undershot bite.

This condition can occur unnaturally, however. Dogs that develop a malocclusion can be treated, but they should never be used for breeding.

BROKEN TEETH

Young dogs will put absolutely anything into their mouths. As they test their new teeth, they will chew away at rocks, pieces of wood, metal, rope – anything. The upshot of this, unfortunately, is that many dogs crack or even break their teeth. This can be a painful experience for the dog. It may be possible to fix it with root canal work but extraction might be necessary in severe cases.

LIP INFLAMMATION

Mouth infections can affect a dog's lips so that the corners become very dry, flaky and chapped. Lips can also become inflamed from the dog chewing rough objects. These conditions can heal themselves, but there are also good softening creams that can be effective.

LIP FOLD INFLAMMATION OR 'COCKER MOUTH'

Some sporting dogs have been bred with a 'flu' or fold of skin on the lower lip. Food and saliva can collect here, which can develop bacteria. This can lead to an inflammation of the folds, which produces an unpleasant odour and can also cause disease. One of the breeds most likely to develop this condition is the Cocker Spaniel, hence the condition's popular name 'cocker mouth'. For this reason the area needs to be cleaned regularly in vulnerable dogs, using Epsom salts dissolved in water.

CHOKING

Dogs should be discouraged from putting small objects in their mouths from an early age. It is something that can be tackled during training at home. They can be dissuaded from playing with small objects by having their toys removed when they do, thus forming a negative association. As they get older, they should also be discouraged from retrieving foreign objects like sticks. It is amazing how many owners still consider this a suitable form of play with their dogs. All it needs is for the stick to break to damage the mouth or throat, and the dog could choke.

The telltale signs of choking are obvious and include:

- distress and choking sounds
- gagging
- agitation
- bulging eyes
- pawing at the mouth
- rubbing the face on the ground.

If you encounter any of these, do the following.

1. Try to stay calm and restrain the dog so you can examine inside its mouth.

2. If you have another pair of hands available, enlist their help. Dogs can lash out and bite when distressed.
3. Hold the upper jaw in one hand and press the upper lip over the upper teeth.
4. Using the other hand, pull down the lower jaw.
5. Use an object like a pen, small spoon or tweezers to pry the offending object out of the mouth.
6. Be careful not to do more harm than good. If, for instance, you see string or fishing line in the mouth, don't pull at it as it may well be attached to a hook, which is in turn fixed to something inside the throat or stomach.
7. If you are unsuccessful in removing the obstruction, head immediately to your vet.

YOUR DOG'S FEET

If your dog starts limping, check its paws first for cuts or objects that have penetrated the pad. Some breeds, such as Spaniels, grow a lot of hair between their toes. This can easily become matted and – in the case of country-based dogs – accumulate grass seeds, dirt and other bits of detritus. If left unattended, seeds in particular can penetrate the skin leading to an infection and the formation of a cyst. It is therefore important to check this area regularly, clipping away any excess or matted hair and removing any debris.

If your dog has a foot injury and you can see a foreign object embedded in the paw, follow these general principles to treat it.

1. Remove objects carefully, always using a pair of tweezers sterilised with a flame or antiseptic.
2. Clean the wound with antiseptic.
3. Objects like thorns may be only partially visible. If so, use a sterilised needle to draw back a small section of skin then pull the object out with the tweezers.
4. If the object is under the skin and not extractable, bathe the foot in salt water until the object emerges to the surface of the skin. If it is embedded too far under the skin, consult a vet.

ANAL SACS

Probably the least pleasant chore a dog owner has to perform is checking its dog's anal sacs. These are two cavities about 5mm in width, which are located on either side of the dog's anus, at the four o'clock and eight o'clock positions. They are lined with cells that regularly secrete a very pungent discharge. In the wild the secretions are used to mark territory, but in domestic dogs they have little use apart from getting attention from other dogs who (for reasons humans find impossible to comprehend) find it attractive.

All dogs need to empty these sacs on a regular basis and often do so while defecating. In some cases, however, the sacs can get blocked and become impacted, which is a very painful condition.

A dog suffering from blocked anal sacs often demonstrates obvious signs of distress. It may 'scoot' its bottom along the ground or lick at the painful area. If it does this you should consult a vet as blocked sacs can become infected and even – in rare cases – cancerous. To make sure things don't get this far, you should check this area regularly during grooming by feeling around the side of the anus.

Sacs that are full feel like a bunch of hard grapes. The dog may react as if in pain when you touch them. You can stimulate the dog to empty them either by inserting a finger behind the blockages and removing them, or by using a piece of cotton wool to squeeze the sac externally. Neither is a pleasant experience for either the dog or the owner. It is best to get a vet to perform this, at least on the first occasion.

❀ ❀ ❀ ❀ ❀ ❀ ❀

As well as keeping a close eye on your dog's condition yourself, you should take it to the vet for a check-up twice a year so that any potential problems can be spotted and treated early. It is good for puppies to get used to being examined by a vet from an early age.

11 | PUSHING THE BOUNDARIES

Until the age of about 14 weeks, your puppy should be confined to its home environment. This is necessary for several reasons. Firstly, the dog hasn't yet developed enough to be able to cope with a long walk. It would get tired easily and might damage its still-developing feet and bones. More importantly, it won't have received all its vaccinations. Without proper protection from the multitude of threats the outside world presents it can't go out. Finally, in the early weeks, it will still be getting used to the sights, smells and sounds of its new home and could find the outside world unduly terrifying.

By around 14 weeks of age, your puppy should be ready to take its first steps out into the wider world and, in doing so, to give its body the greater workout it needs to develop physically. It will still not be able to go far. Small breeds are simply not up to long marches yet, and big breeds, with their vulnerable bones, could do severe harm were they allowed to push themselves too hard physically at this age. Walks should not take the young dog further than a mile or so from the home, and you should start with shorter distances of a few hundred yards or so.

Before you leave the house, though, the dog needs to learn the all-important rules that will dictate the walk. In particular, they must know how to walk on a lead and be able to respond to important instructions from their owners. And this is not all they must be prepared for. The dog's world is going to expand, bringing it into contact with myriad new experiences – all of which it will have to assimilate. The owner needs to be prepared to help the dog deal with this by understanding its body language (this is discussed in the next chapter, pages 167–72).

HEEL WORK

It is in both the dog's and the owner's interests that it learns to walk to heel at the end of a lead.

From the owner's point of view, no one wants to go for a walk with a dog that is constantly straining at the lead. It defeats the object of what is meant to be a pleasant, enjoyable and above all fun exercise.

From the dog's point of view, too, it is bad news. It wants to explore the wider world as freely and enjoyably as possible but if it is constantly being yanked by the neck, or if its owner is repeatedly cutting short its walks, that is simply not going to happen.

If, on the other hand, it learns to walk in harmony with its owner, speeding up and slowing down, stopping, starting and turning at the same time as its guardian, then the walk is going to be the highlight of its day.

Two words of caution, however.

As with so many areas of dog training, the best results will be achieved through a structured, disciplined approach. And this is not something that should be rushed. Invariably, if you allow one hour it will take fifteen minutes to get something right – and if you allow only fifteen minutes, it will take an hour to achieve your goal. So leave plenty of time.

The other thing to be careful of is the use of food rewards. You are going to be using a lot of rewards during the training process, so be careful about the amounts and the frequency. Only give your puppy strips of meat as a reward. The idea of exercise is to improve the dog's health – not damage it.

Here is my step-by-step guide on how to train your dog to walk to heel.

1. CHOOSE YOUR SIDE

You must first choose the side on which you are going to want the dog to walk. For most people this is their left side. (This has developed from the gundog or sporting dog world where most people are right-handed and want to carry their gun under this arm while out hunting. It is easier, and safer, for them to keep their dog to their left.) There is, however, nothing wrong with training the dog to walk on the right. What is important is that once a decision has been made, you adhere to it.

The guide that follows assumes that the owner has their dog on their left. If you want to train your dog to walk to the right, simply reverse the instructions where applicable.

2. BRINGING THE DOG TO HEEL

Working somewhere where there is enough space for dog and owner to walk a dozen or so paces, begin by arming yourself with a piece of food reward. Place this in your left hand then turn your back on the dog. Bring the left hand down along the side of your left leg until it is at the dog's nose level. As you do this call the dog's name and ask it to 'heel'.

If the dog appears at your side as you've requested, give it the food reward and praise it warmly.

If it doesn't appear, don't try again immediately. Leave it an hour or so before trying again. Patience is a virtue.

3. WALKING SIDE BY SIDE

Once the dog has successfully responded to your request to come to heel, you are ready to begin walking slowly. The aim of this exercise is that the dog remains close to your left leg as you move along and that the lead is held loose in your hand.

Begin by calling the dog to heel once more. Then take a couple of steps, using the food reward to encourage it to accompany you. It is important to remember here that the dog is not a mind reader and walking to heel is not something that it would do naturally in the wild. If it strays away from you, encourage it to return to your side with a positive association by giving it some more food reward. Remind it to stay where it is by repeating the word 'heel' as you go. When the dog gets it right and walks at your side for the full distance you want to go, reward him warmly with praise and with one final piece of food reward.

As ever, the main thing to remember is to stay calm and unflappable. No matter how frustrated or cross you might feel at your dog's lack of response, you mustn't show it. The dog will pick up on your anxiety, and that will risk damaging some of the precious trust you have built up. If this happens, it will try to get away from you, which is the last thing you want.

Simply allow things to calm down and start again later.

4. VARY THE EXERCISE
Once the dog has got the knack of walking alongside you, start varying the direction and duration of your practice. Stop and start every now and again. Get the dog ready for the reality of the outside world, where it is going to be travelling on a variety of different routes. When it can deal with this, it is ready for the next bit of training: walking on the lead.

WALKING ON THE LEAD

The lead is the most important piece of equipment your dog is going to wear. It is its safety line, its link to the guardian who is going to protect it from the myriad terrors it is going to face in the outside world. In extreme cases, it might save its life. So it must get used not just to wearing it but also to walking properly and responding to the lead well in advance of its first walk.

Here is my step-by-step guide.

1. SLIPPING ON THE LEAD
Bring the dog to heel, as usual. Lean over and carefully place the loop of the lead over its head. Make sure it fits comfortably. It shouldn't be so tight that it could choke or chaff the dog. Equally it shouldn't be so loose that it might slip off if pulled

on vigorously by the dog. If that happened, the dog might well run away. Place the lead on gently and without any fuss. When it is safely on for the first time, give the dog some warm praise.

2. WALKING ON THE LEAD
Repeat the usual walking to heel exercise, encouraging the dog to stay at your side as normal. If it starts to tug or yank at the lead, stop and calmly stand your ground. The dog needs to learn from the very beginning that tugging matches are simply not acceptable. Resume the walk by once more getting the dog to come to heel. When it is back in position, carry on. Once the dog reaches the end of the walk without having once pulled on the lead, praise it and give it some food reward. It deserves it.

3. LEARNING TO TURN
No walk is ever going to head in a straight line. The dog will have to turn and must learn to do so under your control. These manoeuvres should be practised at home long before the first walk is attempted. Again I am assuming here that most people will walk with their dog to the left. If, however, it is on the right, simply reverse the instructions.

To turn right
Even if it is obvious to you that a turn is required, a dog isn't going to know it unless you make it obvious. And the best way to do that is to use the sort of body language it understands best.

To turn right you should first pivot around, leading with your right leg. Don't lead with the left, as it will cause confusion and problems. The dog will be blocked from turning right and both dog and owner run the serious risk of tripping over each other.

As you are pivoting use a distinctive word, something that the dog will always associate with this manoeuvre. A traditional choice is 'close'. As you turn your body, the dog's head will move with the lead and its body should angle around to the right as well.

To turn left

This is a little more complicated. Begin by gathering up the lead so that there is no slack. This will have the effect of bringing the dog to your side. Now extend the left leg out as far as you can. At this point the leg should be touching the dog's shoulder and neck. Once more choose a distinctive word that you are going to stick to from now on. The traditional one is 'back', for the simple reason that the dog is being asked to drop back.

As you pivot to the left, the dog should naturally drop back. And because your body is now gently applying pressure to the dog's body, it should naturally turn to the left as well. The key here – as always – is that there is nothing sudden or violent about this. It should happen smoothly, seamlessly and calmly. The dog should be reacting naturally to the movements of the owner's legs.

4. STOPPING AND TEACHING THE 'WAIT'

Inside the home you are working in a safe and predictable environment. Outside, the world is going to be anything but safe or predictable, so you must be able to bring the dog to an instant halt. It might be the control that saves its life.

Introducing the 'wait' instruction into heel work is straightforward. As you develop heel work, throw in an occasional sudden stop. Accompany it with a short, sharp – but not too intimidating – instruction to 'wait'.

If the dog does so, reward it. This is something that needs a positive association. Then carry on with the walk. Introduce stops like this at regular intervals from now on.

5. SIMULATE THE REAL WALK

With all the elements in place you can now make use of whatever space is available to extend the length of the walk. This is the time to begin simulating the demands of what will be the real walk. Throw in all the different elements – the turns, the wait – mixing them up so that the dog doesn't know what is coming next. Keep it guessing – and thinking – all the time. Work towards a situation where there is no tension on the dog's lead at all. Aim for such a well-coordinated relationship between you and your dog that someone watching you would conclude that you must be joined by an invisible line. When you have achieved this, you are ready to head out into the world.

THE FIRST WALK

It is always worth taking a moment to think about things from a dog's perspective. This is certainly the case when it comes to the first walk.

The dog sees itself as a member of a functioning pack, so when it steps out into the world with that pack, it is like its ancient ancestor the wolf going out on the hunt. This is another of the key moments when the leader, the alpha male, stamps his authority on his subordinates. The alpha decides when the pack goes out on the hunt. Before the pack leaves, it checks to see whether it is safe to leave the den. And when it decides the coast is clear, it is the alpha who leads the way out into the world – and then chooses the direction in which they are to head.

The domestic dog attaches the same importance to its walk. For that reason it is vital that the owner takes charge of each aspect of that walk, just as the alpha within the wolf pack does.

By now the basic foundations should have been laid. The dog should have formed a close bond of trust with you. It should also have learned to walk to heel. So it should be ready to follow you into the wider world, secure in the knowledge it will be safe as it does so.

The first walk is going to be a big moment for both you and your dog. You want it to be a positive association for the dog to remember. Choose a day that is going to provide an experience that is as enjoyable as possible. Make sure you have plenty of time and, if at all possible, that the weather is good. Work only within the limits you feel are safe. You should constantly be asking yourself 'Do I feel happy and in control?'

If the answer is yes, carry on. If the answer is no, take a step back and continue with the basic training at home until you are more comfortable.

When the moment does come for the first walk, be sure to follow the following principles closely.

1. PREPARING TO LEAVE HOME

The key thing to remember here is that you must lead from the front. You must be the first person across the threshold and you must be the person who decides the length, duration and direction of the walk. Have this at the forefront of your mind throughout.

Call the dog to heel as normal and slip on the lead. Start heading towards the door.

Dogs are smart and will quickly pick up on the fact there is something different about today's routine. If it suddenly gets agitated or tries pushing in front of you, stop. As usual, this should be done calmly, without any histrionics or raised voices. Once things have calmed down, bring the dog to heel once more and try again.

2. THROUGH THE DOOR

Make sure you are the first to cross the threshold. If the dog tries to force its way past you, stop. Return to the house, bring the dog to heel and start again. This principle is important so it must be learned by the dog from the outset.

Once you have got through the door properly, you can relax a little. This is, after all, a thrilling moment for your dog. You can let it enjoy itself.

The dog should begin walking to heel. Don't worry too much if it gets a few steps ahead. That is the point of having a lead with a length of leather or rope on it. Only act if there is any significant tension on the lead by simply calling the dog to heel. When it does this, reward it warmly with praise. Complying with your request when there is so much excitement going on around it is worthy of praise.

3. TAKING DIRECTION
The dog must learn at this early juncture that it is not in charge of any aspect of the walk. The next crucial moment comes at the boundary of the home where dog and owner are suddenly faced with the option of heading in one of several directions.

If the dog begins heading off in one direction, execute a smart about turn and start walking the other way. If the dog begins veering off, change direction again. Keep repeating this until the dog has understood that it is not in charge of the walk. Once again, your aim is to keep the dog thinking. In this case, it is going to be asking 'Where are we going?' By taking control you will help it reach the conclusion it needs to reach: 'It's not for me to decide.' And you will have helped it to start exercising self-control. As with all good teaching, students must be allowed to make the right decisions for themselves.

4. BUILD IT INTO AN ENJOYABLE EXPERIENCE
The first walk should be a gentle introduction for both dog and owner, and it should continue this way for the next few

days. Owners should build up their confidence with the controls they have developed so far. The dog should become used to the idea that when it steps out into the world with its guardian it always returns safely home.

The dog should not be let off the lead until it is at least nine months old and has proved that it responds well to instructions while walking on the lead, as well as in all aspects of its behaviour at home. This step has to be planned carefully too. If rushed, it could lead to dire consequences, with the dog running off and getting lost. Literally, it must learn to walk before it can run.

In any case, this new phase of going for walks on the lead should be enjoyed by both dog and owner. An owner can derive immense pride and joy from leading a dog that is light on its feet and responding well to requests. You only have to look at the way a young dog walks along wagging its tail and happily exploring the exciting new world opening up around it to understand that it is having fun.

FEAR OF NOISES ON THE WALK

The outside world is full of strange, surprising and sometimes very loud noises. They are shocking for humans let alone dogs. At least we can rationalise what they are and where they are coming from. Dogs cannot.

At home we can teach our dogs to ignore loud noises by exuding calm and a lack of panic. But as the dog begins to venture further and further away from the home, this isn't always going to be enough. Everything from cars and motorbikes to alarms and aeroplanes overhead can upset a dog. In the most extreme cases, the experience can leave them nervous and anxious for a long period, even for life, so it is important to tackle this head on.

A dog is never going to understand what a burglar alarm or a fire engine's siren is, or tell the difference between the sound of a firework or a backfiring car. All it can know is that the sound isn't threatening its safety. And the only person who can tell it this is you, its owner.

When you reach the road, wait there. When the dog reacts to the first car or lorry passing by, the key thing is that you don't mirror its panic. Simply let the vehicle pass and the sound fade, then reassure the dog simply with a 'good dog' and a piece of food reward. Don't make a fuss over it, however.

This process should then be repeated. Wait for the next vehicle, let it pass and again reward the dog afterwards. Slowly it will get the message that you aren't worried by what is going on here. And nor should it be.

Repeat this procedure to help it get used to any other loud noises you commonly encounter on your walk, until the dog is able to stay calm while you are out.

GETTING USED TO THE CAR

Once the dog is fully immunised, you may want to travel further afield. To be able to achieve this with your dog, you will need it to be comfortable travelling in your car. Again, this is something that needs to be tackled with care and planning.

Dogs can easily form phobias about travelling in cars. Their reactions can vary from shivering and generally cowering in the car to completely over-the-top panic, leaping around and barking. Neither is good for the dog or the owner, who has to drive while all this is going on. So for the sake of both of you – and for the safety of other road users who could be affected – the dog needs to get used to car journeys.

The puppy's first experience of travelling in a car will probably have come at eight weeks when it moved home. It may not need to travel again until it goes for its vaccinations at the vet's. Yet it is important that it becomes used to the environment inside the car, and to travelling short- to medium-range distances in it before that point.

As with so many other areas, the key is making a positive association. This is something that can be done as an extension of the familiarisation process that's already going on. As the dog begins to explore the outside world around the house, you should encourage it to spend time around the car as well.

Your first trips with the dog should be relatively short affairs, perhaps just a drive around the local area without stopping anywhere. Make the trip after a meal and after the dog has had a good play and is relaxed.

Have some newspaper, a towel, a blanket and some wet wipes to hand in case the experience proves too much for the dog. Car or motion sickness is very common among dogs, particularly young ones. You should also have something comforting, perhaps a blanket or a toy that makes the association a happy one.

If you have another dog who is a good traveller, you could bring it in the car with you. If you have a dog that is not a good traveller, however, it shouldn't be brought along on the trip. Bad habits rub off on each other. Finally you should have someone else accompany you, preferably someone whom the dog knows and is comfortable with.

There are several places you can put the dog. The important thing is that it is comfortable and secure. Note that it should never be put in the passenger seat alongside the driver. You can opt for:

- a harness in the back seat;
- a cage at the back of the car;
- a cardboard box if it is a small puppy;
- or, if necessary, put the dog in the foot well of the passenger seat.

It isn't hard to imagine what an overwhelming experience this is going to be for a young dog. It has been familiarising itself slowly with unfamiliar sights and sounds for a few weeks now, but the journey it is about to take is going to be a sensory overload, filled with myriad new sights, sounds and smells. So be prepared for it to have a strong reaction.

If the dog becomes distressed when you start the engine and move off, the passenger should offer a reassuring stroke of the hand. It shouldn't be overly dramatic, just a reassuring presence. Equally if there is a physical reaction – if the dog is sick or soils the car – there should be no reaction. Just clear up the mess and head home then wait a few days before trying again.

If, however, all goes well, when you arrive home, immediately take the dog to the garden or toilet area, where it will probably need to go. Praise it warmly when it does this, laying the seeds for a good association.

If the dog suffers persistently from motion sickness, you should consult your vet about travel sickness tablets, which are highly effective. If you don't do this, the dog's bad association with the car is simply going to get worse and the problems will become self-perpetuating.

❧ ❧ ❧ ❧ ❧ ❧ ❧

Controls are vitally important when you take your dog into the outside world. In the next chapter, we will discuss ways in which you can tell what your dog is thinking and feeling and can therefore help it to deal with unfamiliar situations more easily.

12 | UNDERSTANDING YOUR DOG'S BODY LANGUAGE

It's obvious that dogs need help from their owners when walking near roads or other potentially dangerous spots. But the dog will face subtler terrors too, ones that the owner may not appreciate. While a dog will not be able to verbalise the fears it is feeling, it will be signalling its discomfort, however. To help the dog's transition into the wider world, it is crucial to understand how it communicates its feelings.

Our dogs may not be able to communicate with us in our own language, but they are certainly able to give us a range of powerful signals using their own, highly developed body language.

It is a language all dogs will learn during their early development. With a movement of their ears or tail, or with a change in body position, the young dog will learn how to send a message that another dog will be able to read immediately. As the young dog matures it's important that we learn to recognise these signals too.

YOUR DOG'S SIGNALS

Dogs use an array of tools to deliver their body language messages. We only have to look at two extremes to see this.

🐾 If we look at a dog that is signalling fear, for instance, we will see anxiety in its eyes, its ears pinned right back, there will be tension around the mouth and the body will be slouched backwards in a defensive posture. Finally its tail will be between its legs.

🐾 Equally, if a dog is standing upright, with an inquisitive, happy look in its eyes and no signs of tension in the body and its tail wagging, it is a clear signal that the dog is happy.

But between these two extremes there are subtleties that owners need to understand. And to do that we need to understand how it uses different aspects of its physicality to express itself.

EARS

In the wild, the wolf uses its ears as a major part of its defence – and attack – system. It is able to twist them so as to pick up sounds, whether those of potential attackers or prey. The ears also allow wolves to interact as a hierarchy. If a wolf's ears are pricked, it is signalling that its interest is aroused in something. A relaxed state of mind is signalled by the ears being turned to the side while still slightly pricked.

Our dogs use their ears in a similar way. The key positions are:

🐾 ears pricked forward – alert, interested;
🐾 ears slightly pricked to the side – relaxed;

🐾 ears held back – respect;
🐾 ears pinned right back – fear, submission.

EYES

They say that eyes are the mirror of the soul and this is certainly true with dogs. You can see a whole range of emotions by looking into a dog's eyes – everything from strength and confidence to fear and pain. And you can always be certain that what you see is what the dog is feeling. Dogs, unlike humans, don't lie.

Generally speaking, the main signals are:

🐾 wide, bulbous eyes – stress, fear;
🐾 fixed gaze – strength, confidence;
🐾 glare – threat, aggression;
🐾 soft eyes – relaxed.

TEETH

In the wild, teeth are the ultimate weapon in the wolf's armoury. They know they can kill with them, so it is not surprising that they are used as a powerful signal.

The amount of teeth shown varies according to the amount of information it wants to convey. If a wolf wants to issue a general warning, it will lift its lip just enough to show a tiny percentage of its teeth. If this message doesn't get through, it will show slightly more teeth. This will continue until it has rolled back its lip to reveal a whole set of teeth and gums. In conjunction with a glare of the eyes, this conveys a message that is unmistakable. At the opposite end of the emotional spectrum, the teeth can also be used to demonstrate contentment. As many owners will know, a dog can physically smile, often with a curl of its upper lip and a revealing of its teeth.

A domestic dog taps into this same vocabulary to signal its moods and feelings, and it can use the whole foreface and mouth area to get its message across.

The Side of the Mouth

The jaw works in conjunction with the teeth to provide extra subtleties of signalling. The more forward the side of the mouth, the more aggressive the expression is. If it is pulled back it is more defensive.

Foreface

The foreface is the area around the nose and mouth. By manipulating this area, the dog is able to deliver a range of expressions, from a smile to a crunched-up face that is a sign of aggression.

STANCE

As a well-designed running machine, the wolf has a very balanced frame. It uses this to send subtle signals, pushing it forward to show potential aggression, pulling it back to show submission, in particular towards its superiors within the pack. Our dogs do this too.

HACKLES

The dog's ability to make its hair stand on end is essentially a mechanism for making itself look bigger. Again it is something acquired from the wolf, whose thick coat allows it to add inches all over to make itself look more intimidating. Instinctively the wolf will always try to avoid confrontation by scaring off any threats. Yet equally, raising the hair can signal joy.

TAIL

The tail tells you a great deal about the dog's personality, its confidence level, its status and its mood. It will also tell you a great deal about its reaction to the world around it. This is the ultimate signal for a dog, and one that is unique to its species.

There are four key positions:

- When a dog is in a relaxed and happy state its tail should hang at a downward angle, without any obvious tension in it. This indicates the dog is comfortable with the world.
- If the tail is tucked beneath the dog's tummy, it is a sure sign it has been frightened by something.
- When a dog is out on a walk, the tail extends horizontally from its rear, with a level carriage.
- The higher the tail carriage, the higher the dog's confidence and its perceived status. In the wild an alpha wolf will carry its tail almost at right angles to its back.

The tension – or lack of it – in a dog's tail is also a strong signal. In the normal position, the dog's tail hangs limp, like a flag at half mast. But if that tail is high, say at 90 degrees to its back, and rigid as well, then it is a pretty clear indication of aggression.

And every dog owner knows that a wagging tail is a sign of a heightened state, usually a pleasurable one.

YOUR DOG'S COMMUNICATION WITH OTHER DOGS

The original dogs – wolves – were perfectly equipped to communicate with each other. Their physical make-up was designed to give them the ability to get the message across to their peers quickly and efficiently. They had a balanced-shaped skull, pricked ears and uniformly-shaped forefaces and they all looked alike so there was little room for misinterpretation or confusion.

After 14,000 years of human breeding, however, the dog has evolved in myriad different directions. There are now thousands of diverse breeds, many of them shaped to meet the tastes and practical requirements of human society rather than those of the canine world. The upshot of this, however, is that dogs cannot read each other as well as they used to. And this can cause problems, especially when dogs that are unknown to each other interact.

So as owners prepare to guide their dogs on walks in the outside world where they will come into contact with other animals, it is important to spare a few moments to understand some of the limitations their pets may face. Some breeds have restrictions in terms of what they can and cannot signal. Their physical structure may limit them. This is potentially a problematic area and it is important that we, as owners, are aware of this.

EARS

In trying to understand why some dogs attack other dogs, it's worth thinking about how they see each other. For instance, if a dog is showing another dog what it perceives to be a lack of respect by not dropping its ears, this may be taken as an antagonistic signal. But what if the offending dog simply cannot drop its ears? A Springer Spaniel, for instance, cannot drop and raise its ears like other breeds.

In some countries it is common to crop a dog's ears so that they are fixed in a permanently pricked position. To other dogs this is signalling a state of permanent alert, which is always going to leave them on their guard.

Your dog may react with confusion and even aggression if it comes across other breeds whose ears won't drop. It needs to learn that there are subtleties to their species, and that not all dogs look like those they have been used to in the litter and at home.

EYES

Wolves have eyes that are proportional to the face and allow them a wide range of expressions. Breeding has removed some of these options for certain dogs, however.

Dogs with very small eyes, or those whose eyes are hidden behind overhanging hair, like Old English Sheepdogs or Maltese Terriers can have difficulty communicating with other breeds, because the other dogs simply can't read the signals they are giving.

Through breeding, some breeds, such as Pugs, Boxers, Chihuahuas, Cavalier King Charles Spaniels and Bull breeds have very wide and bulbous eyes. To another dog this may give the impression that the dog is stressed or aggressive, and it may mean it won't want to play with it in a social situation.

FOREFACE

The foreface is one of the most expressive areas of a dog's face. The area between the eyes, down along the nasal passage to the snout and along the side of the jaw provides them with a range of signalling options. A tiny movement here can allow them to bare their teeth, wrinkle their nose or even to smile. Because of the number of muscles at play, the area is immensely flexible. But again, if breeding has produced a dog that cannot manipulate its foreface, then problems and misunderstandings arise – for both the signaller and the recipient.

For example, dogs need to be able to see frowns and grimaces, but breeds such as the Sharpei have developed so many layers of folds on their faces that other breeds are going to find it very difficult to spot these subtleties.

King Charles Spaniels and Boxers have had their nostril area bred shorter and shorter. This means they are now denied the array of signals available with a full face.

If the foreface can't do this, then none of these signals are available. If a dog is slightly upset, it can signal this with a slight, almost imperceptible curl of the lip. If it is more angry it will show more teeth. If it is really angry, it will show a full set of teeth. If the foreface can't do this, the dog won't be able to give warning signs to other dogs when it is getting angry and may have to resort to direct confrontation rather than threats.

STANCE

Dogs with very broad chests, such as Boxers, are not nature's norm. Their overdeveloped chests and broad shoulders make them look top heavy, like the canine equivalent of Arnold Schwarzenegger. As a result they appear threatening to other dogs. Their back end is also lighter, making them look as if they are leaning forward, which adds to this effect.

Breeds such as the Pekingese, on the other hand, are confusing. With their long coats and short legs, it's hard to see where the body begins and ends. You don't know whether they are standing up or lying down. Their flat faces only add to the uncertainty other dogs will feel when meeting this type of breed. They won't know whether to play with it or eat it! Again, owners should bear this in mind when they begin introducing their dogs to other breeds.

HACKLES

People often see the raising of the fur along a dog's back as being associated with aggression, but it can also be signalling an entirely different emotion – joy. So if you have a dog whose fur is standing up all the time – such as a Pomeranian – be aware that this can confuse other dogs. Equally, be aware that dogs such as Dalmatians or Chinese Crested, with smooth or furless coats, don't have the option of raising their hackles, and this is something that limits their ability to communicate with other breeds.

TAIL

The tail is a feature that has been changed a lot by generations of human breeding. As a result it can be the cause of a great deal of confusion and misunderstanding amongst dogs. In particular, owners should be aware of communication problems with the following tail types.

Long tails

Some breeds, such as Basset Hounds and Dachshunds, have been bred with such short legs that their tails look disproportionately long. The natural position for other breeds is to carry the tail slightly below the horizontal but if these dogs did this their tails would be trailing along the ground. To be comfortable, they carry their tails slightly higher. You know that this is normal compensation for what is in effect its disability, but other breeds of dog could easily misinterpret this as a challenge.

Curled tails

Some breeds have been altered so as to have very curved tails. Examples include the Elkhound, the Basenji and the Pomeranian. It is easy to see how this would be confusing to another breed encountering one of these dogs for the first time. They won't be sure whether it is signalling that it is relaxed or making a threat, and the results could easily be a bad reaction.

Docked tails
The docking of tails is now largely banned in European countries, except for in very special circumstances. However, there are many older dogs who have had their tails docked. While they are still able to use their stumps to a degree, they are nowhere near as efficient or as easily understood as a full tail, especially from a distance. Another dog may get completely the wrong end of the stick when it first sees a docked dog. By the time it gets up close and sees the reality of what it is signalling, it may be too late. In breeds where other features are limited as well, such as Spaniels, with their floppy ears, a docked tail only adds to their disadvantaged status.

❀ ❀ ❀ ❀ ❀ ❀ ❀

Some dogs are handicapped by a combination of all these factors. Consider the poor Old English Sheepdog, for instance. Another dog coming into contact with this breed for the first time will encounter what looks like a giant kitchen mop. They can't see eyes, ears or a foreface. They can't see a tail. All they see is a broad-chested animal covered in fur. It isn't even clear that it is a dog, so it is no surprise that other dogs often misread this breed in particular.

As you take your dog out for walks in the outside world, you must help it to deal with communication problems when it meets other dogs, and, as always, your own reaction will be key to this.

INTRODUCING DOGS TO OTHER BREEDS

Because dogs are such intelligent creatures, they will do all they can to survive in this world. They want to avoid confrontation and will do their best to achieve this. So, for instance, when it is growing up a Dachshund puppy will learn that a high tail carriage is not necessarily a signal of dominance within their breed. Given their short legs and long tails, to drop the tail to the normal, slightly drooped position would leave it dragging uncomfortably along the floor. When they meet other dogs, of course, they will encounter animals who don't see things the same way. And this is where problems may set in.

This is not to say two breeds can't play together, but they must have time to overcome their initial confusion. Dogs operate according to the old saying 'Beware instant friends', so when they go out into the world patience must be the byword.

Because dogs of different breeds will confuse each other with their different signalling, it is helpful for puppies to be given the chance to get to know a wide range of other dogs and given time to assimilate with each other. One way to do this is via good-quality socialisation or puppy classes. Puppies meet each other at such classes and learn to be comfortable in each other's presence. Yet, even here, owners must be aware that things aren't necessarily going to work out immediately. Don't rush things. Give the dog time.

CANINE CONFRONTATIONS

Socialising and interacting with other dogs and, more to the point, other 'packs', is an unnatural act. In the wild, packs instinctively avoid each other and mark out their territory specifically to ensure this never happens. In the human world, of course, it isn't possible or desirable to avoid other dogs. Dogs need to exercise and – unless you are lucky enough to live in a particularly isolated corner of our overpopulated planet – this will inevitably result in their meeting other dogs and their owners.

As we have seen, dogs can send out confusing and dangerous signals to each other when they meet on their own. But when they meet with their owners, there is an additional ingredient that can inflame the situation. Your dog may react aggressively, so it is important that you are prepared to deal with this potential problem.

The key is to practise 'cross packing' – that is, getting your dog used to encountering other dogs and their owners. When you approach another dog and its owner, you need to show calm, consistent leadership, living up to Kipling's old saying 'If you can keep your head while those about you lose theirs …' Here is some more specific advice.

🐾 Keep walking with your dog on its lead, trying to give the other dog as wide a berth as possible.

🐾 Don't acknowledge or even look at the other dog and its owner as you walk past.

🐾 If your dog walks past without acknowledging or confronting the other dog, when you reach a reasonable distance away, reward it with food.

As ever, it is all about making a positive association. And the more often you do this, the sooner it will cease to be a problem.

Of course you are not the only element in the equation here and it is quite possible that the other owner has less control and understanding of their dog than you do. So, unfortunately, you have to be prepared for the possibility that another dog may act aggressively towards you.

The key to dealing with this situation is, again, to remain calm. In addition you should do the following.

🐾 Remove your dog from the situation as quickly and quietly as possible.

🐾 Don't make a huge fuss or engage in a shouting match with the other dog and its owner. This will only inflame the situation and panic your dog further.

🐾 Don't pick up your dog unless the danger is too great not to. Even if you have to, try to remain calm. The way you deal with the situation sends out important information, both to your dog and to the dog causing the problem.

🐾 Don't become part of the problem. Your dog will not see you as weak for removing yourself from this situation. The need to survive over-rides all others.

🐾 If your dog walks away without over-reacting, reward its behaviour with a small treat.

🐾 🐾 🐾 🐾 🐾 🐾 🐾

Being alert to the signals your dog gives is particularly important when you are out on a walk. After a while, as you get to know each other better, this will become second nature. Always remember that your dog will be reading your signals as well. If it senses that you are scared or stressed by a situation, then it will be as well. But if you react with calm acceptance of external stimuli, your dog will too.

13 | MONITORING THE PHYSICAL CHANGES IN YOUR PUPPY

The dog's first year is a steep upward curve of development. The first six months of a puppy's life will see it passing through its most intense growing spell.

At three months, depending on their size and breed, dogs will weigh somewhere between 20 and 30 per cent of their adult weight. By the time they reach nine months, they will have grown to such an extent they will now weigh well over 80 per cent of what they will weigh when they reach full maturity at around two and a half years old.

The rates of growth vary widely. Small breeds, unsurprisingly, grow faster than large breeds so that some dogs have reached well over 90 per cent of their adult weight by the time they are nine months old. For the large and giant breeds of dogs, the real growth spurt comes between three and five months. They still continue to put on weight after this but the rate slows and becomes more steady as they head towards maturity.

The dog's dietary demands during this phase will be great – but so too will the risk of it becoming overweight.

WATCHING YOUR DOG'S WEIGHT

As with humans, weight problems can come about all too easily. All a dog has to do is eat too much and do too little exercise. The calories that aren't burned off on the daily run or walk will be stored in the body in the form of fat. In some cases obesity is down to the metabolic make-up of the dog, but mostly it is down to the owner failing to be responsible about food and/or the dog's exercise regime. There are a number of common mistakes that owners make.

- ❖ Feeding the dog poor-quality leftovers from their own meals.
- ❖ Giving them regular snacks or treats, particularly human ones such as chocolate.
- ❖ Overusing food rewards in training, thereby encouraging the dog to be constantly on the look-out for tidbits.
- ❖ Failing to give the dog sufficient exercise.

Between 40 and 50 per cent of our dogs are overweight. As with humans, it is becoming an epidemic that could have disastrous consequences.

Dogs that are carrying too many pounds tend to live shorter and less healthy lives than those who are at the ideal weight. The extra pounds place an increased burden on bones and joints as well as the heart. The dog may also be less well equipped to resist infections.

And once a dog does get overweight, a downward spiral can set in. They can become lethargic and lose interest in playing or taking any form of exercise. This in turn will lead to a further deterioration in their health.

According to some vets, weight problems can be genetic. Among those breeds predisposed to being overweight are the

Beagle, Basset Hound, Cairn Terrier, Cavalier King Charles Spaniel, Dachshund, Labrador and Retriever.

If left unchecked, weight problems can lead to a whole host of diseases and conditions. These include:

- diabetes
- liver diseases
- strains on the heart
- heat intolerance
- a deterioration of coat and skin condition
- reduced resistance to infectious diseases
- respiratory problems
- arthritis
- hip and elbow dysplasia
- spinal disc problems
- ruptured joint ligaments.

Given this, it is vital that you monitor your dog's weight. The simplest way to do it is at the vet's, where standing on the scales should be part of the regular visit. You can then compare its weight with breed standards, to make sure it is on target. But it is also important that you body score your dog at its annual check up.

HOW TO MONITOR YOUR DOG'S WEIGHT AND CONDITION

With dogs prone not just to obesity but to so many other related diseases and disorders, it's vital that you maintain a close eye on their physical condition throughout their life. This is particularly important during the first crucial six-month phase of their development.

It is not just obesity that owners should be concerned about, of course. A dog that is seriously underweight can develop problems that will at best handicap it later in life or, at worst, shorten its life considerably.

Keeping a close check on your dog's condition means much more than running an eye over them every now and again. It demands a regular evaluation of their weight and condition so as to give you a body score.

HOW TO BODY SCORE YOUR DOG

One of the benefits of having developed a good relationship with your dog early on is that it will allow you to touch it. This will be invaluable when body scoring, as it requires that you examine it thoroughly all over.

The main checks are on the ribs and the tail base. Run your fingers over them and assess how easy it is to feel the bones. The other key thing to look for is the shape of the abdomen. The best way to assess this is by standing over the dog so you are looking directly down on it.

There are five categories of body condition.

1. Emaciated

A score of one is given to a dog that is thin to a dangerously unhealthy degree. Its ribs are easily felt and it has no fat covering. Its other bony points are also easily found. Its tail base is prominent and there is no tissue between the skin and bone. From above it is easy to see a pronounced and severe tuck in the abdomen. It's obviously clear in this case that the dog needs further veterinary attention.

2. Underweight

A body score of two is given to a dog that is underweight. Its ribs are easy to feel and there is only minimal fat cover. The tail base is raised and bony and there is little tissue between the skin and the bone. In a puppy over six months, there will also be a tuck in the abdomen when it is viewed from the side. When looked at from above, it will have a distinct hourglass shape.

3. Ideal

This represents the ideal body condition, and scores three on the body scoring scale. The ribs are easily felt but there is a thin belt of fat between the skin and bone. The bony points are also easily felt with a healthy amount of fat covering them. With dogs over six months, there is a well-proportioned waist visible from above, while there is a tuck in the abdomen when viewed from the side.

4. Overweight

A dog scoring four is defined as being overweight. Its ribs are hard to feel underneath a significant layering of fat. The tail base is thickish and lies beneath a similar amount of tissue between the skin and bone. It is still relatively easy to feel the bony parts of the body but they too are covered by layers of fat. In animals over six months there is no tuck in the waist when viewed from the side and the back is wider when looked at from above.

5. Obese

A dog that is obese is categorised by a score of five. Its ribs will be very hard to feel under a thick covering of fat, as will its tail base. When viewed from the side, older dogs will have no waist as such; instead there will be a bulging and slightly pendulous belly. When inspected from above, the dog's back will be significantly broader than normal. If in doubt, as ever, consult your vet.

DEALING WITH WEIGHT PROBLEMS

Dealing with dogs that are marginally under- or overweight is a relatively straightforward matter. A reduction in the amount of food they eat and a corresponding increase in the amount of exercise they take should do the trick. The only caveat is that the transition should be made gradually, over a period of a week or so, or you risk delivering a shock to the dog's system.

In addition to this owners must cut out snacks, stop feeding leftovers and get the dog out of the habit of demanding tidbits constantly.

Treating a dog that is seriously over- or under-weight is another matter, however. This is something that should be done in conjunction with a vet. They will be able to advise you on the best way to tackle the problem and in particular they will be able to recommend the most appropriate diet.

Veterinary science has made such advances in recent years that there are now dozens of very specific diets, geared to particular needs. These include low-calorie diets for weight loss and high-energy/high-calorie diets for weight gain. Work with your vet to find the right one for your dog.

DENTAL DEVELOPMENT

A dog's dental development is geared to its ancient role as a predator. Like its wolf ancestor, a puppy will first have a set of deciduous or baby teeth that will allow it to educate itself in the ways of the pack. By the age of seven months or so these baby teeth will have been replaced by a full complement of adult teeth. In the wild, these teeth arrive in time for the young wolf's first ventures out with the pack and its role as an apprentice hunter.

Typically, the development process will go as follows:

🐾 At three to four weeks, the first deciduous or baby teeth arrive, in readiness for the puppy to start interacting and playing with its siblings.

- ❧ By the end of the sixth week all the deciduous teeth are in place. Normally a puppy has 28 of these baby teeth.
- ❧ Between three and five months of age, the dog passes through the next phases of development and the baby teeth are replaced by the permanent incisors, canines or cuspids and finally the molars.
- ❧ At five to six months, the permanent canines break through.
- ❧ By the end of the seventh month the last molar in the lower jaw is in place. A properly developed dog should now have 42 teeth, including 12 incisors, 4 canines or cuspids, 16 premolars and 10 molars.

These processes are normally straightforward, but see page 145 for advice on what to do if your dog has problems with its teeth.

PUBERTY

Puppies can enter puberty quite early in life, and are able to impregnate or get pregnant, so if your young dog is going to encounter any other dogs – either in your house or garden or while out on walks – it is essential that you watch for the signs of puberty and take steps to protect it.

MALES

The male dog's testes are made up of a mass of coiled tubes, which are stored in the scrotum. When puberty arrives, they will begin to produce sperm and will continue to do so throughout a dog's life, although in smaller quantities as the dog gets older.

The testes develop in the puppy, fixed to the scrotum by a ligament. As this ligament contracts, the testes drop through into the scrotum. The testes should be descended within the first few weeks of the puppy's life and can often be felt, but as the dog grows fat around the scrotum they can be less easy to find until the onset of puberty at around four months.

As the dog reaches this age, it is important to check that it has two descended testes – although owners shouldn't panic if only one drops to begin with. Cases of retained testes are not uncommon, with the second testicle dropping as late as 18 months. As usual, however, if there is any doubt, consult a vet.

A male dog reaches puberty at a young age. In theory, this means that it could start fathering puppies from the age of five or six months old, but it is not a good idea to let young males breed. First and foremost, of course, letting your dog roam free impregnating every in-season female it encounters is going to fill the world with even more unwanted dogs. But there is a behavioural aspect to this as well. A young dog that is allowed to mate freely can develop aggressive and dominant tendencies. This, once more, goes back to the wild, where only the alpha male is allowed to mate. A dog that is allowed to mate when and where it wants will naturally assume it is a leader, which will have major behavioural repercussions. So at this early stage in life, owners should be vigilant in keeping their males under control at all times.

FEMALES

Females tend to enter puberty within a month or so of developing fully physically. For this reason, smaller breeds – who reach their adult size that much quicker – will have their first season much earlier than larger breeds. A dog from a small breed can have its first season as early as five months old. Giant breeds, on the other hand, may not reach puberty until as late as two years of age.

Owners should check female dogs from the age of six months onwards. Often the dogs themselves will offer telltale signals. For instance, the dog might start showing more interest in its hygiene, cleaning and licking itself. Nature is telling her that she is vulnerable and needs to look after herself.

The surest way to check is by examining the vulva. Using a white tissue, touch around the vulva area. If there is any 'pinking' or any red discharge then you can be pretty certain she is coming into season. A female is extremely vulnerable during this period, not just to unwanted conceptions but also to diseases such as Pyometra, infections of the uterus. As well as keeping the female dog isolated from males and other dogs in general, it is vital that she is kept clean and clear from infection.

NEUTERING

Deciding whether to castrate a male or spay a female dog is a big decision, but one that many owners make. I have no objection to it, in particular in one of the following situations.

- The dog is going to be an assistance dog, that is, a guide dog or other kind of human helper. If the dog is a female in particular, the possibility that it will be unavailable to its disabled owner while it carries and raises pups has to be removed.
- Many rescue organisations insist on neutering dogs that come to them. This is understandable because in many cases they will know nothing about the dog's background.
- Dogs with hereditary problems.
- Dogs whose responsible owners have made a firm decision that they are not going to breed.

On the other hand, there are some circumstances in which neutering is not recommended.

- Neutering for behavioural reasons is the worst thing you can do. Such problems are often to do with the dog's inability to carry out its perceived role as leader of its domestic pack. These issues should be treated by relieving the dog of its status as leader, not by creating an even more wounded animal. Neutering only creates an even more insecure dog and can make it more panic-stricken and aggressive.
- If an owner intends to show a dog. Kennel Club requirements may stipulate that a dog must be 'entire' or that it is able to reproduce.

❖ If you are uncertain whether to breed or not. It's irreversible so you have to be sure.

❖ ❖ ❖ ❖ ❖ ❖ ❖

The next stage of life, when your dog becomes an adolescent, will present a whole new set of pleasures and challenges. But if you have laid the foundations of good behaviour in the first six months of the puppy's life, you should have a strong mutual understanding forming the basis of a rewarding and happy relationship with each other.

CONCLUSION

Just like its ancestor, the wolf, the dog has a lengthy childhood in animal terms. It has to be this way because a puppy has a great deal to learn during this period. In the wild, the events of the first six to nine months are all leading up to the moment when the young wolf is allowed to take its first steps into the wider world by joining the pack. Its apprenticeship is over and it is ready to enter a new phase.

For the domestic dog, too, the end of its first six months marks a major landmark. It is now able to move around in the wider world. Soon it will be ready to roam free on its own, to go for progressively longer walks, and to run off the lead in environments where there are potential threats and dangers all around. By the age of nine months, your dog should be becoming more responsible and ready to widen its horizons. It is an adolescent now, rather than a puppy, and if you have completed its basic training well enough, it can be allowed more freedom.

The work you have done during the early months will have been vital in preparing your puppy for this moment. If you have got it wrong, then more problems await you. If you have got it right, however, a wonderful new world lies in front of you. In the days, months and years ahead, your relationship with your dog will blossom into something truly special.

FURTHER INFORMATION

While I hope this book has covered all the main subjects that will concern an ordinary dog owner, there is no way it can claim to answer every conceivable question. With so many breeds and so many minor ailments and conditions in existence beyond those I have outlined in the preceding pages, that is inevitable. The good news, however, is that there are a number of respected institutions and bodies which between them can provide answers to 99.9 per cent of the issues an owner is likely to face. And if they don't know the answer, they can certainly refer you to someone who does.

I have drawn on the expertise of many of them myself in the compilation of this book. Listed below is a selection of some of them, along with the major international points of contact that will act as ideal starting points for dog lovers around the world.

CONTACTS IN THE UK

British Small Animal Veterinary Association
Woodrow House
1 Telford Way
Waterwells Business Park
Quedgeley
Gloucester
GL2 2AB
Tel: (01452) 726700
www.bsava.com
Enquiries: administration@bsava.com

British Veterinary Association
7 Mansfield Street
London W1G 9NQ
Tel: (020) 7636 6541
www.bva.co.uk
Enquiries: bvahq@bva.co.uk

Dogs Trust (formerly the National Canine Defence League)
17 Wakley Street
London
EC1V 7RQ
Tel: (020) 7837 0006
www.dogstrust.org.uk
Enquiries: info@dogstrust.org.uk

The Kennel Club of Great Britain
1–5 Clarges Street
Piccadilly
London
W1J 8AB
Tel: (0844) 463 3980
www.the-kennel-club.org.uk
Enquiries: info@the-kennel-club.org.uk

OVERSEAS CONTACTS/KENNEL CLUBS

AUSTRALIA
Australian Capital Territory
Dogs A.C.T.
PO Box 815
Dickson
ACT 2602
Tel: (02) 6241 4404
www.actca.asn.au
Contact: info@dogsact.org.
au

New South Wales
Dogs NSW
PO Box 632
St Marys
NSW 1790
Tel: (02) 9834 3022 or 1300
728 022 (NSW only)
www.dogsnsw.org.au
Contact: info@dogsnsw.org.
au

Northern Territory
Dogs NT
PO Box 37521
Winnellie
NT 0821
Tel: (08) 8984 3570
www.dogsnt.com.au
Contact: admin@dogsnt.
com.au

Queensland
Dogs Queensland
PO Box 495
Fortitude Valley
Qld 4006
Tel: (07) 3252 2661
www.cccq.org.au
Contact: info@
dogsqueensland.org.au

South Australia
Dogs SA
PO Box 844
Prospect East
SA 5082
Tel: (08) 8349 4797
www.dogssa.com.au
Contact: info@dogssa.com.au

Tasmania
Tasmanian Canine Association Inc.
PO Box 116
Glenorchy
Tas 7010
Tel: (03) 6272 9443
www.tasdogs.com
Contact: admin@tasdogs.com

Victoria
Dogs Victoria
Locked Bag K9
Cranbourne
VIC 3977
Tel: (03) 9788 2500
www.vca.org.au
Contact: office@dogsvictoria.org.au

Western Australia
Dogs West
Corner Warton and Ranford Roads
Southern River
WA 6110
Tel: (08) 9455 1188
www.dogswest.com
Contact: k9@dogswest.com

BELGIUM
Fédération Cynologique Internationale
Place Albert 1er, 13
B-6530 Thuin
Belgium
Tel: 071 59 12 38
www.fci.be

BRAZIL
Confederaçao Brasileira de Cinofilia
Tel: (24) 9279 1915
www.cbkc.org
Contact: cbkc@uninet.com.br

CANADA
Canadian Kennel Club (CKC)
200 Ronson Drive
Suite 400
Etobicoke
Ontario
M9W 6R4
Tel: (416) 674 3699
www.ckc.ca
Contact: information@ckc.ca

CZECH REPUBLIC
Ceskomoravská Kynologická Unie
Jankovcova 53
CZ-170 00 Praha 7
Tel: 234 602 274
www.cmku.cz
Contact: cmku@cmku.cz

DENMARK
Dansk Kennel Klub
Parkvej 1
2680 Solrød Strand
Denmark
Tel: (56) 18 81 00
www.dansk-kennel-klub.dk
Contact: post@dansk-kennel-klub.dk

FINLAND
Finnish Kennel Club
Kamreerintie 8
Finland 02770 Espoo
Tel: (9) 887 300
www.kennelliitto.fi
Contact: fihs9cd9@ibmmail.com

FRANCE
Société Centrale Canine
155 avenue Jean Jaurès
F-93535 Aubervilliers
France
Tel: 01 49 37 54 00
www.scc.asso.fr
Contact: contact@scc.asso.fr

GERMANY
Verband für das Deutsche
  Hundewesen (VDH)
Westfalendamm 174
44141 Dortmund
Germany
Tel: (0231) 56 50 00
www.vdh.de
Contact: info@vdh.de

HUNGARY
Magyar Ebtenyésztök
  Orszagos Egyesülete
Tétényj ut 128/b-130
Budapest
H-1116
Tel: 0036 1 208 2300
www.meoe.net

IRELAND
The Irish Kennel Club
Fottrell House
Harold's Cross Bridge
Dublin 6W
Tel: (01) 453 33 00
www.ikc.ie
Contact: ikenclub@indigo.ie

ITALY
Ente Nazionale della
  Cinofilia (ENCI)
V. le Corsica 20
20137 Milano
Italy
Tel: 02 700 20 324
www.enci.it
Contact: info@enci.it

JAPAN
www.jkc.or.jp

NETHERLANDS
Raad van Beheer
Emmalaan 16–18
NL-1075 AV Amsterdam
Tel: 20 664 4471
www.kennelclub.nl
Contact: info@kennelclub.nl

NEW ZEALAND
New Zealand Kennel Club
Prosser Street
Private Bag 50903
Porirua 5240
Tel: (04) 237 4489
www.nzkc.org.nz
Contact: nzkc@nzkc.org.nz

NORWAY
Norsk Kennel Klub
PO Box 163
Bryn
0611 Oslo
Tel: 21 60 09 00
www.nkk.no
Contact: info@nkk.no

POLAND
**Zwiazek Kynologiczny W
Polsce**
Zarzad Główny
Al. Jerozolimskie 30 lok.11
PL-00-024 Warszawa
Poland
Tel: (022) 826 05 74
www.zkwp.pl
Contact: zg@zkwp.pl

PORTUGAL
**Clube Português de
Canicultura**
R. Frei Carlos, 7
1600-095 LISBON
Portugal
Tel: 217 994 790
www.cpc.pt

SPAIN
**Real Sociedad Canina de
España**
Calle Lagasca 16
28001 Madrid
Spain
Tel: 914 264 960
www.rsce.es
Contact: administracion@
rsce.es

SWEDEN
Svenska Kennelklubben
S-163 85 Spånga
Sweden
Tel: 8 795 30 30
www.skk.se
Contact: info@skk.se

USA
**The American Kennel Club
(AKC)**
260 Madison Avenue
New York
NY 10010
USA
Tel: (212) 696 8200
www.akc.org
Contact: info@akc.org

United Kennel Club
100 E Kilgore Rd
Kalamazoo
MI 49002-5584
USA
Tel: (269) 343 9020
www.ukcdogs.com

**The Westminster Kennel
    Club**
149 Madison Avenue, Suite
    402
New York
NY 10016
USA
Tel: (212) 213 3165
www.westminsterkennelclub.
    org
Contact: write@wkcpr.org

INDEX